ALL ONE IN CHRIST?

All One in Christ?

GILBERT W. KIRBY

KINGSWAY PUBLICATIONS
EASTBOURNE

First published 1984

ISBN 0 86065 283 1

Printed in Great Britain for
KINGSWAY PUBLICATIONS LTD
Lottbridge Drove, Eastbourne, E. Sussex BN23 6NT by
Richard Clay (The Chaucer Press) Ltd, Bungay, Suffolk.
Typeset by Nuprint Services Ltd, Harpenden, Herts.

To Connie
my devoted companion and counsellor
for over forty years, who is ‘worth more
than rubies’

Contents

Introduction

I seem to recall there was, in my youth, a popular song the refrain of which was 'The more we are together the happier we shall be'. To be honest, I think it was originally a German drinking song and as far as I know it had no spiritual overtones! Those words, however, have frequently come back to me over the years and somehow have taken on new meaning.

It is a fact that ever since the Second World War the historic churches have been very much taken up with the subject of unity. The ecumenical movement found expression in the formation of the World Council of Churches in 1948. Those who have had and still have serious misgivings about the ecumenical movement have nevertheless given serious attention to the question of unity. Although for a century or more Evangelical Alliances had existed in different countries of the world, it was not until 1952 that the World Evangelical Fellowship—a linking together of national fellowships and alliances—came into being. This desire for togetherness has also found expression at the local level in the proliferation of evangelical fellowships and associations. The movement in this direction received a great deal of impetus as a result of Dr Billy Graham's crusades in 1954–5. Christians who had come together in support of these crusades tended to want to stay together. In the following decade the Evangelical Alliance arranged two united communion services in the Royal Albert Hall in London; this was yet another expression of the desire to come together across denominational barriers.

The Keswick Convention 'for the deepening of spiritual life' has for over 100 years been an annual rallying point for Christians but within the past few years similar interdenominational gatherings have come into being up and down the country–the Filey Christian Holiday week now located at Skegness, the Dales, the Downs, Spring Harvest, Royal Week, to mention but a few. All this points to a felt need on the part of Christians right across the denominational spectrum to get together.

One cannot but feel that this is a movement of God's Spirit. It is at the same time an answer to the prayer of our Lord for his disciples. There is a growing wish to be one and to be seen to be one. This desire has percolated down to the level of the local church in that almost everywhere you find a warmth that was not so obviously there a few years ago. The ice is slowly melting. Christians are beginning to act as brothers and sisters. There is a greater familiarity among God's people–even to the extent that we now address one another by our Christian names!

In this book we endeavour to take a look at the subject of unity from different angles and we shall no doubt come to the conclusion there is still a long way to go. The 'unhappy divisions' are still there but often in a different form. Denominational differences are less marked but Christians will tend to polarize over such issues as the charismatic movement, the doctrine of the church and the interpretation of prophecy. It is our prayer that what we have written may highlight the joy of 'togetherness' without overlooking the problems involved in achieving it. All too often one comes across Christians whose concept of togetherness amounts to a takeover bid! True 'togetherness' does not necessarily mean uniformity, but rather mutual respect and acceptance. There will always be issues over which equally spiritual people will have to agree to differ.

I should like to acknowledge my indebtedness to my good friend, Jean Wolton, who has typed the manuscript for me, and to my many friends and colleagues in the Evangelical Alliance, the London Bible College and in the churches in which I have served. It has been a privilege to work happily with all these people over many years and to experience spiritual unity in action.

1

In Praise of Togetherness

'My wife's not a very good hostess... our friends never feel really welcome when they first arrive...' 'My husband's always putting his foot in it and I get so embarrassed when...'

Have *you* ever come across couples who as a matter of course speak disparagingly of one another? It is certainly not pleasant to be caught in the crossfire of a family tiff, especially when you discern deep-seated bitterness and resentment between the people concerned.

On the other hand, it is a real delight to be a guest in the home of a happy and united family. There is a relaxed atmosphere; no one feels threatened. There is no power struggle. The husband does not make snide remarks calculated to humiliate his wife; the wife does not display an aggressive attitude towards her husband; and the children do not have to be constantly nagged but clearly respect their parents. As a guest you are made to feel 'one of the family'.

Why are some families like this while others are quite the opposite? The family is a divine institution and only functions properly when the Maker's instructions are followed. The roles of husbands and wives and parents and children are clearly set out in

Scripture and we overlook this fact at our peril. God does expect husbands to shoulder their responsibilities and wives to respect their husbands. He does look to children to obey their parents but equally he warns parents against nagging their children. It is impossible to have a happy family if every member is at cross-purposes with every other. Members of the family must know their respective roles. That does not mean husbands should be dictators lording it over their cowed wives or that children should be seen and not heard. It does not imply that women should be seen solely as mothers with no thought of their doing a job outside the home or being persons in their own right. I am not advocating a return to the days when children addressed their fathers as 'Sir'. Nevertheless, there are ground rules as far as home life is concerned and if we flout them we court disaster. A home where Jesus is acknowledged should surely bear a different stamp from a godless home–the stamp of unity.

Anyone who has listened to the demanding cry of a young baby must be aware that as far as he is concerned the whole world revolves around him: everyone else is there to serve his interests and meet his needs. It is only as we grow up that we come to see that the interests of others have also to be considered. Sadly, however, there are those who never seem to learn this lesson. Even as adults, they still feel they must always be 'Number 1' and this inevitably creates tensions. Unity depends on our willingness to defer to one another rather than browbeat one another.

Most of us spend the greater part of our lives 'at work', and relatively few have jobs where individuals are left to their own devices. We are, of course, not unmindful of the fact that for many married women 'work' consists largely of household chores, bringing up a family and making ends meet. Such 'divine service' is not to be lightly regarded, although here we are thinking now particularly of those of us who 'go out to work'.

Generally, people work in close proximity to other people whether it is in an office, in a shop, on the factory floor or on the staff of an educational establishment. We probably work there for a minimum of thirty-five hours per week and most men and some women have a 'working life' that spans nearly fifty years. How important it is therefore that we should be happy at our place of work, and get on well with our colleagues. The fact remains, however, that a large number of people find their working conditions almost intolerable. There is bitchiness, jealousy, backbiting. Meaningful relationships scarcely exist, and Monday mornings are not looked forward to.

What is the answer? There is no truly satisfactory answer apart from a change of character, new birth. Christian teaching makes for tolerance and mutual respect and forbearance. Those who have tasted divine forgiveness recognize, or should do, the need to be forgiving and the importance of togetherness. But even apart from a spiritual rebirth, Scripture teaches certain basic principles that we cannot afford to overlook. If working conditions are to be at all satisfactory employees must respect employers and employers must be understanding of employees. Work is to be seen as something worth doing and not just a necessary evil. A man or woman who is both happy at home and also enjoying good working relationships at his place of employment has much for which to be grateful.

Apart from work, many people come together in order to follow their leisure-time pursuits. In any community there are clubs and societies catering for many and varied interests. Those who join such groups often forget their differing backgrounds because they share something they consider to be of paramount interest. Sadly, though, from time to time disagreements occur and often resignations follow.

For Christians there is a particular area where they are brought into close contact with their fellow men and women–in the church. Here one would fondly imagine there would be no problems. After all, are we not all Christians and have we not been taught to love one another? We all know from experience, though, that it is not quite as simple as that. Even when people have been converted, they may still be very far from the goal of spiritual maturity. They may be indwelt by the Spirit of God yet the fruit of the Spirit is slow to become apparent in their lives. In the best of churches there are a few people who find it difficult to get on with their fellow believers. The church at Philippi was a very happy fellowship but even there, there were a couple of women who got on each other's nerves! Paul and Barnabas had at one time a sharp difference of opinion and parted in angry dispute. And Paul certainly did not always see eye to eye with Peter!

It seems that wherever you have people you have problems!

But why is it so difficult for people, even Christians, to get along together? What are the factors that create tensions among us?

First, there are environmental factors. Home backgrounds differ and upbringing varies enormously. We have all been conditioned to some extent by the input we received in formative years, and find it hard to accept ways other than our own.

There are also differences of culture. These may be most pronounced in the case of those of another race but even within Britain there are a variety of subcultures. Even our sense of humour is to some extent conditioned by the subculture to which we relate.

Temperament is probably the greatest single factor affecting our relationships. We sometimes classify people as either introverts or extroverts. The introvert tends to withdraw within himself while the extrovert is sociable and outgoing. Four centuries before Christ a Greek philosopher, Hippocrates, put forward the theory that there are four basic temperaments–the sanguine, the choleric, the melancholic and the phlegmatic. Sanguine people live in the present and enjoy life. They are warm, buoyant and generally cheerful, although they tend to be guided by the heart rather than the head. We could perhaps put the Apostle Peter into this category. Choleric people are quite different. They are self-determined and unemotional, inclined to be hard almost to the point of cruelty. In contrast, melancholics know the heights as well as the depths. Sensitive and idealistic, they often excel in the fine arts and in creative thinking. The phlegmatic person sometimes appears lazy because of his or her reluctance to become involved. Nevertheless, phlegmatics are usually dependable and efficient and work well under pressure.

Of course, no one person fits exactly into these categories but it is undeniably true that we all differ in temperament, thus helping to explain why getting on with other people can be such a problem. In view of all this diversity, it is not surprising that people of the same nationality, even fellow citizens of the kingdom of heaven, do not see eye to eye. However, the Bible makes it very clear how we should handle these differences—'submit to one another out of reverence for Christ' (Eph 5:21). If relationships with those around us are strained, life becomes miserable. The art of living with others is one that all of us have to learn. The poet who said 'No man is an island' was right.

One of the most hackneyed words used in Christian circles is 'fellowship'. Different organizations in the church are termed 'fellowships'—the Young People's Fellowship, Women's Fellowship and such like. Fellowship, however, in New Testament terms represented something very much deeper than we usually experience today. It meant partnership, sharing one's goods, sharing one's life. It was this that made such an impact on the pagan community in the first century. Basic to getting on with people is the practice of sharing; to establish a relationship calls for a willingness to share someone else's interests. Some people have few real friends because they really only want to talk about themselves and what they have been doing. They are not really interested in the other person, and what he or she has been doing. To establish a good relationship with someone requires a willingness to show an interest in that person and in turn that means being a good listener. Ability to enter sympathetically into the interests of others is a first principle when it comes to forming good relationships.

Graciousness is another vital ingredient if we want

to get on with other people. There are those whose proud boast is 'I'm John Blunt. I call a spade a spade and I don't mind whether I offend or please'. Folk like that would no doubt thrive on a desert island but they are hardly likely to be appreciated in normal society. However, we are not suggesting that our goal should be popularity. The world is littered with those the Bible describes as 'men pleasers'. Chameleon-like, such people immediately take on the colour of their surroundings; they have no mind of their own, no clear-cut convictions and the result is that they have little to contribute. In contrast, Jesus was one of the most outspoken of men who ever lived, yet people 'spoke well of him and were amazed at the gracious words that came from his lips' (Lk 4:22). What matters is *how* we put things across. So often there is a breakdown in relationships because of a lack of sensitivity. We need to consider the feelings of others when we speak.

Appreciation is another quality that contributes towards good relationships. Expressions of appreciation, provided they are genuine, are of enormous worth. So often people are discouraged and even disgruntled because no one ever passes on to them a word of encouragement. We take one another for granted. If husbands were more ready to express appreciation of their wives' culinary efforts it would act like a tonic. If children occasionally expressed their appreciation of their homes, parents would be greatly heartened. If the director acknowledged with gratitude the typist's efforts she would no doubt be encouraged. The last thing that is called for is flattery that is insincere. That is very different from the expression of genuine pleasure in the good qualities or work of another.

There is perhaps one word that more than any other holds the secret of good relationships—whether in the home, at work or in the fellowship of the church. This word is 'caring'. We get on well with others if we show we really care for them. The Apostle Paul underlined this in his first letter to Corinth. Speaking of the church as a body, he said that 'its parts should have equal concern for each other. If one part suffers, every part suffers with it; if one part is honoured, every part rejoices with it' (1 Cor 12:26). It is caring that counts. Of course, we will only care for people if we bother to get to know them and begin to share their interests. Because some churches are so large this is a real problem, especially if we only attend Sunday services. No one can get to know and really care for more than a limited number of people, and in order to try to deal with this problem many churches have formed fellowship groups that usually meet mid-week in someone's home. Thus fellowship is broken down into units of manageable size.

Jesus told his disciples to be as wise as serpents but as harmless as doves. This surely means we must use our wits and devise ways and means of fostering a spirit of unity within the community to which we belong. Sometimes we tend to leave it all to other people when *we* ought to be taking the initiative. Being harmless as doves implies watching what we say, not blurting out remarks likely to cause unnecessary strife.

Christians need to heed the beatitude that refers to peacemakers—'for they will be called sons of God'. We occasionally come across people who could more accurately be described as troublemakers—those who stir up strife and display a belligerent attitude. It is significant that one of the qualifications for a church leader is that he should be 'temperate, self-controlled ...not violent but gentle, not quarrelsome' (1 Tim 3:2–3). There are undoubtedly Christians who love to get embroiled in controversy, who love to start an argument but Scripture makes it clear that such people are not suited to leadership positions.

Togetherness matters. Whether in the home or in the local church, it is to be cherished. The psalmist was right when he said: 'How good and pleasant it is when brothers live together in unity' (Ps 133:1). If unity is to be preserved there must be both openness and humility. When we feel unity is under threat, then we must act quickly and seek to make peace. We must never allow estrangement to remain, still less to grow. Immediately, as soon as we are conscious of a broken relationship, we must act by taking the initiative to mend it. Jesus made this clear when he dealt with the logical implications of the sixth commandment (Mt 5:21–30).

2

Our Lord's Prayer

In recent years no question has received so much attention, in all sections of the Christian church, as that of Christian unity. Sermons are preached; books are published; articles are continually written on this topic. Furthermore, no one can afford to be disinterested in the subject since it is so prominent in the New Testament itself. It looms large in the teaching of our Lord, but it is also prominent in the Acts of the Apostles, and in the New Testament epistles. It is, however, quite clear that not all Christians mean the same thing when they speak about unity. For some, unity is closely akin to, perhaps even identical to, uniformity.

Therefore we need to inquire as to the nature of the unity envisaged by Christ. What is the unity he willed for his people? In answering these questions we need to look particularly at Jesus' words recorded in John's Gospel—'that all of them may be one' (17:21). At the same time we need to know the context in which this prayer was offered, and this teaching given.

No prayer uttered by Jesus has been preserved in such detail as this one, and it might rightly be termed 'The Lord's Prayer'. It was the prayer that Jesus prayed on the night on which he was betrayed. He had already met with his disciples in the Upper Room and they had taken the bread and the wine together. After singing one of the psalms of David they left the Upper Room, went through the side streets and passed the city gates over the brook Kidron, on towards the Garden of Gethsemane. No doubt our Lord continued his teaching as they went on their way beneath the light of a full moon. It was the privilege of these same disciples later to hear Jesus at prayer.

In the opening verses of chapter 17 our Lord is praying chiefly for himself (v.1–5). Here we have the most wonderful expression of his personal communion with the Father. In the next few verses he begins to pray for his own, those whom God had given to him out of the world (v.6–10). The first actual reference to unity comes later when he prays 'Protect them by the power of your name—the name you gave me—so that they may be one as we are one (v.11). In subsequent verses he refers to the subtle attacks of the enemy who will be eager always to break up the essential unity of his own people. Christ goes on to pray more especially for their sanctification, that they may be kept in the truth (vv.17–19). It is then that we begin to learn something about the nature of the unity that he envisaged for his disciples (v.22). The prayer concludes with the plea that they may be where he is and may behold the glory that the Father has given to him (v.24).

The question that we would ask is: 'Who is envisaged in this prayer?' Is it merely a prayer for those who were immediately around him at the time, or does it encompass his disciples in every generation? The answer to that is clear. Jesus says: 'My prayer is not for them alone. I pray also for those who will believe in me through their message' (v.20).

This prayer, therefore, encompasses *all* believers in *all* ages. We must emphasize, however, that it is the unity of true believers that Christ has in mind in his prayer. He is clearly praying for a particular group of people who are described in some detail. They are those who have been given to him by God (v.24); they are people who have been separated from the world (v.16); they are the people on whose behalf he said he sanctified himself (v.19). They have recognized that he was sent by God and they have believed in him.

So we are left in no possible doubt as to who is included in this prayer. It is a clearly defined group of people whom we might well describe as 'true believers'. This is not a prayer for the world, nor is it a prayer for all who 'profess and call themselves Christians' but it is a prayer that covers all who have been truly 'born again', redeemed people who together make up the church which is his body.

We must now ask the further question: 'What kind of unity does our Lord have in mind for these people?' The answer to this lies in verse 22 where we learn that the unity between Father and Son within the Godhead is to be the pattern for the unity of believers—'that they may be one as we are one'.

This is not merely oneness in will and purpose, but oneness in nature or essence. Thus his prayer is for complete harmony of nature, a fellowship in spirit. Obviously a unity of this dimension is only possible among those who already enjoy a personal relationship with Jesus—those who 'participate in the divine nature' (2 Pet 1:4). It is a staggering thought that the unity about which Christ prayed is seen as being comparable to the unity that exists eternally between Father and Son within the Godhead. Clearly, this is something very different from the external organizational unity that is so often discussed these days. Here is something that is first and foremost spiritual—a unity of essence.

In likening this unity to that existing within the Godhead, our Lord drew attention to the fact that it was also to be a unity in diversity. The mystery of the Trinity consists of the fact that there are three Persons but only one God. Although they are of the same essence, they are distinct as Persons, thus it is perfectly clear that Christ did not envisage uniformity for his people but rather a unity existing in diversity. This, of course, is borne out by the fact that, as Paul points out in his letter to the Corinthians, there are many different spiritual gifts that equip servants of God for specialized ministries. Furthermore, it is significant that in the New Testament no blueprint is laid down as far as church order is concerned. Obviously, Jesus was not primarily concerned that there should be uniformity in such matters.

A further matter that emerges from this prayer regarding the nature of the oneness of God's people is that he assumes that this oneness is already in existence but needs to be preserved. It is not something that has to be created or manufactured, but it is something that has to be maintained. This thought, as we shall see in Chapter 3, is expressed elsewhere in Scripture. It is quite beyond the powers of men to create the sort of unity that Christ had in mind when he prayed for his disciples. He prayed to his Father to preserve a unity that was already in existence: a unity that is the creation of God's Holy Spirit. Such unity is something to be seen by the outside world and will help to commend the gospel. Clearly Christ envisaged a church that would be both vitally and visibly one.

In stressing the fact that this unity was basically spiritual in nature, we would at the same time point out that it was to be essentially practical in its outworking. It was a unity that would cause the world to believe. The world can only understand spiritual unity in so far as it expresses itself in action. True spiritual unity is a most practical thing. It is not something academic and theoretical. Acts 2 begins with the statement that 'They were all together in one place', and the chapter ends by telling us—'All the believers were together and had everything in common. Selling their possessions and goods, they gave to anyone as he had need' (vv.44–45). It was when the church was united in this way through the Holy Spirit that blessings came, and we find that 'the Lord added to their number daily those who were being saved' (v.47).

The unity for which Jesus prayed is spiritual, visible and practical. All too often such words are regarded, at least by implication, as being mutually exclusive. This, of course, is the devil's lie. A truly spiritual person is a truly practical person. True spiritual unity is bound to express itself in works of mercy and compassion. It is when the church enjoys this spiritual unity and expresses it in such action that an impact is made on the community.

3

Common Ground

The theme of Christian unity is particularly prominent in Paul's letter to the Ephesians. The Apostle speaks mainly about Christian unity in chapter 4, but we cannot divorce this chapter from the preceding chapters. The teaching given in chapters 1–3 is the basis and the background of what follows in chapter 4. The unity of which he speaks is for those who have responded to the message expounded in the earlier chapters.

We note that these Christians were not called upon to manufacture this unity, to create it, or to try and arrive at it, but to 'keep' it. In other words, the unity was already in existence. Christians simply have to be careful that they do not allow anything to interfere with it. It is 'the unity of the Spirit'—a unity that is produced by the Holy Spirit and by him alone. As Paul has shown earlier, it is a unity that overrides racial barriers and brings together both Jews and Gentiles in Christ Jesus. The 'dividing wall of hostility' has gone for those who are united by a common trust in the Lord Jesus Christ.

Paul then proceeds to enumerate some of those things that all true Christians have in common. We all belong to one body. The church is not really divided–it cannot be. There is a spiritual oneness that unites all who are truly born again. The true church embraces believers in all the different branches of the church. In every denomination there are purely nominal Christians but there are also those who truly know Christ as Saviour and Lord and these belong to the body of Christ. In the sight of God there is but one church made up of all who have been redeemed.

In the book of Acts we have accounts of how several different people became Christians. The circumstances varied greatly. The Ethiopian eunuch was poring over Isaiah chapter 53, earnestly trying to discover the true meaning of what he was reading. God arranged for Philip the evangelist to pass that way and to enlighten him. The result was he turned to Christ there and then and was baptized. Paul was once a bitter opponent of Christianity and God broke into his life dramatically as he travelled along the road to Damascus. Lydia was a God-fearing woman who opened up like a flower when she first heard the gospel preached. The Philippian gaoler was frightened out of his wits when he called upon the name of Christ. The way these different people came to faith was so different yet in each case their conversion was the work of the Holy Spirit.

We have all had our eyes opened by the same Spirit. God has not dealt with all in precisely the same way but in every case it has been a work of the Spirit. 'No-one can say "Jesus is Lord", except by the Holy Spirit' (1 Cor 12:3). As Christians we have all been 'born again' by the same Spirit, we are all led and indwelt by the same Spirit, and given power by the same Spirit.

There is 'one hope' before us all. We all look forward

to the same future—there is only one heaven to attain. We may choose to keep ourselves in watertight compartments down here, but there it will be different—there are no denominations in heaven. So as Christians we share a common hope—we all alike look for the coming of Christ and to enter fully into his kingdom.

We all serve the one Lord, and here is the fundamental secret of our unity. We all acknowledge the same Lord. The church is one because Christ is one. We sing 'The church's one foundation is Jesus Christ her Lord'; all who are truly united to him are united to one another. In a wheel the spokes may be divided at the circumference but all meet at the hub. So Christians, if they have Christ as their centre, find their unity. The nearer they get to him the nearer they get to one another.

We all subscribe to one faith. This refers to the 'body of truth' as contained in the Bible. We may differ on certain details of interpretation, but basically there is 'one faith'—'the faith that was once for all entrusted to the saints' (Jude 3). Christians are not free to believe just what they like; they must all subscribe to the same fundamental truths. In Christ, the living Word, we find our oneness as Christian believers.

We all acknowledge one baptism. This does not refer primarily to water baptism, but to our baptism in the Spirit. Paul wrote to the Corinthians–'For we were all baptized by one spirit into one body'. All Christians are indwelt by the same Holy Spirit and are thereby initiated into the body of Christ.

There is one God and Father of all—we are all his children by virtue of our 'faith in the Lord Jesus Christ'. Therefore, we are brothers and sisters. Notice how he is described here: God above all, God through all, and God in all (Eph 4:6). 'Above all' reminds us of his sovereignty; he alone is supreme. 'Through all' reminds us that he works through us all to achieve his purposes in the world. 'In all' reminds us of his indwelling presence in each one of us by his Spirit to comfort and to bless.

There is one unity, though, that we cannot have—that which is bought at the expense of truth (2 Jn 7–11; Gal 1:9). There cannot therefore be any unity with those who do not accept the Bible as their yardstick—with those who preach 'another gospel'.

Here then is the basis on which our unity rests. But what part do we have in all this? The answer is that we have to make every effort to keep the unity of the Spirit. Although our unity is the creation of God the Holy Spirit, the responsibility for maintaining it is in our hands. But how do we do that?

First, we need to recognize that in all of us there is an obstinate streak, that to a greater or lesser degree we are all angular. Paul shows us the way—'Be completely humble and gentle; be patient, bearing with one another in love' (Eph 4:2). Pride and intolerance militate against true unity.

The New Testament abounds in examples of the sort of attitude we should have towards one another if we are to enjoy true unity. First, we must be ready to bear one another's burdens. There is one burden that each of us must bear alone and that is our personal accountability to God, but there are many other burdens that we can share with one another. There is a variety of ways in which we can do this. One of the most obvious is by prayer. It is important that our prayers should be informed, and thus we should be in the closest possible contact with those for whom we have promised to pray. This may apply particularly to Christians serving overseas as missionaries. They send home prayer letters in order that we may bear their burdens at the throne of grace and pray for them intelligently.

When we pray for people we instinctively think of ways in which we can follow up our prayers, and so bearing one another's burdens often means practical action of one kind or another.

Caring for each other is another practical expression of our unity in Christ as we have already seen. Caring for one another means that we take an intelligent interest in what is going on, without, of course, becoming busy-bodies. In the context of the local church this will involve us in visiting others and in writing appropriate letters on certain occasions. We ought also to have outlets for expressing our care on an inter-church basis.

Contributing towards one another's needs is yet one further way of demonstrating our oneness in Christ. An example of this can be seen in the collection that the Apostle Paul organized for the poor saints at Jerusalem. Although we may be living in a welfare state, there are still opportunities of expressing our love and care for one another by giving financial and material support. Most Christian churches have a benevolent or fellowship fund. In some cases they donate to it when they meet at the Lord's Table. Even if poverty is not the problem it once was, there are still people in need. Many old-age pensioners and others would greatly appreciate a parcel of groceries at

Christmas or at other times in the year.

There is a very great deal of emphasis upon the need for Christians to show hospitality in the New Testament. Our homes, if they are Christian homes, ought to be 'open homes'. Sometimes we tend to invite only our intimate friends, or our relations, into our homes, but they should be open to the stranger, the visitor, the overseas student, and other people who might otherwise be lonely. We need to remember the apostolic injunction—'Do not forget to entertain strangers, for by so doing some people have entertained angels without knowing it' (Heb 13:2).

Many Christians are somewhat critical of the idea of confession being made to a priest at an appointed time. However, we shall be ready to confess our faults to one another on an appropriate occasion (Jas 5:16). This must never be something artificial or organized, but it can be of untold blessing when Christian people open their hearts to one another and confess their shortcomings. We only do this, in fact, when a warm and loving relationship exists. In such circumstances confessing to one another enhances unity rather than detracts from it.

We are told to be ready to 'speak the truth in love'. As Christians, being members of the same family, we ought to be on the most intimate terms, so that we can feel free to speak to one another about things that disturb us without running the risk of giving offence. If there are things in another Christian that are offensive to us, then we must be ready to go directly to the person concerned and tell them, always of course 'in love'. Sometimes it means admitting we were wrong and saying 'sorry'. In our dealings with Christians in other branches of the Christian church nothing is lost by being frank. Where differences exist we must be prepared to face them fairly and squarely.

The writer to the Hebrews said, 'Let us consider how we may spur one another on towards love and good deeds' (Heb 10:24). We are all very human, very much 'in the flesh'. There are times when we may get despondent, or depressed, or discouraged, and it is at such times that fellow Christians can be a tremendous source of strength and encouragement.

Christianity has been described as 'love in action'. Because Christian unity is so precious, it must be lifted out of the realm of the theoretical and academic and find expression in practical ways.

4

Unhappy Divisions

In one of our older hymns, we glibly sing:

We are not divided,
All one body we,
One in hope and doctrine,
One in charity.

But is it true? How can we really sing such words when we have a multiplicity of different denominations, each claiming to be representing authentic New Testament Christianity? How can they all be right? Should we not be ashamed of our 'unhappy divisions'? Is there any hope of bringing these different branches of the church together? Are they willing to lose their identities? Why do we perpetuate denominations in the twentieth century that arose out of doctrinal disputes occurring several centuries ago? How should we regard denominations? Should we brush them aside as being no longer relevant or should we see them as regiments in the same army? These are some of the questions that arise in people's minds, particularly among the younger generation.

The ecumenical movement has now been in existence for nearly forty years and during that time there have been numerous discussions on these questions and debates on the subject of church unity. A few attempts have even been made to unite different denominations although these mergers have not, on the whole, been totally successful.

But do we need bother about the subject? Should we not get on with the work God has given us to do in our local church and leave other Christians to do the same? That sounds reasonable enough until we remember Christ's prayer in the Upper Room: 'That all of them may be one' (Jn 17:21).

Also, despite Christ's plea for oneness, it is still a fact that young Christians with neither knowledge of church history nor denominational background have to decide between the competing claims of a whole host of different denominations. 'Can't I just be a Christian?' they ask. 'Do I have to have an additional label such as Anglican or Methodist or Baptist?'

To help answer these questions, it is necessary to examine how the different denominations originated. To do that in depth would take a whole volume but I will try to sketch briefly how our 'unhappy divisions' came about.

Even in the apostolic age there were forces at work that threatened the unity of the infant church. First, there were those who introduced false teaching. There were the Judaizers who tried to insist that Gentiles who embraced the Christian faith should first submit to Jewish religious practices; and there were the Gnostics who claimed to have a superior knowledge and understanding of Christianity and who combined a certain amount of Christian doctrine with speculative philosophical ideas of the day.

Controversy also arose over the person of Christ. Some held that a divine power descended *on* Jesus and enabled him to do the works of God, while others believed that all the fullness of the Godhead dwelt *in* Jesus and that this was a 'mode' of God's self-revelation. Another dispute that split the church for a time was sparked off by Arius, a presbyter of Alexandria living in the fourth century. He taught that Christ had come into being out of non-existence, that 'once he was not' and that 'he was created and made'—teaching that is still propagated today by Jehovah's Witnesses. It was to try and deal with this particular form of false teaching that the Emperor Constantine convened the first General Council of the church at Nicaea in AD 325.

In addition to the numerous controversies that vexed the life of the early church, there was increasing rivalry between the cities of Rome and Constantinople. The Roman Emperor Constantine, when he came to power recognized that Rome was too far away to handle the Eastern problems of the Roman Empire, and on May 11th 330 he dedicated the 'new Rome' and called it Constantinople. However, the Bishop of Constantinople began to compete with the Bishop of Rome for the primacy of the Christian church and gradually the Greek East began challenging the Latin West. Pope Leo I was the first Pope to claim universal supremacy in the church but such a claim was countered in 588 when John, the Patriarch of Constantinople, assumed the title of 'Universal Bishop'. Over the next few centuries tension between Rome and Constantinople grew and things came to a head in 1054 when, in the words of the historian, Edward Gibbon, 'The rising majesty of Rome could no longer brook the insolence of a rebel, and Michael Cerularius [the Patriarch of Constantinople] was excommunicated in the heart of Constantinople by the Pope's legates'. So here was the first big break in Christendom, and it was not long before others followed.

Like Leo I, when Hildebrand became Pope in 1073 he declared that everyone on earth, from the emperor down to the humblest peasant, must acknowledge his supremacy. For the next two centuries papal power was at its height, but eventually groups of Christians started to protest about the errors and superstitious practices they saw in the Catholic church. They were the Paulicians in the Black Sea area, the Bogomites in Bulgaria and Bosnia, the Beghards in the Netherlands and later the Albigensians in southern France and the Waldenses in northern Italy. There were those within the Catholic church too, who spoke out against its policies and practices, among them an Englishman, John Wycliffe, 'the Morning Star of the Reformation'. All this slowly led up to the next big division in Christendom—the Reformation which set out to restore the church to its original simplicity and to rid it of excessive ritualism and superstition.

In many countries in Europe there was growing discontent with the Roman Catholic church during the sixteenth century. In Germany, Martin Luther spearheaded the revolt, and in Switzerland there was Ulrich Zwingli and John Calvin. In a very short time Protestantism became firmly established in northern Europe including Britain. The Reformers saw themselves as leading men back to the beliefs and practices of the apostolic age rather than propagators of new doctrines. Protestantism took on different forms in different countries. In England, for example, King Henry VIII proclaimed himself the 'Supreme Head of the Church of England', while in Scotland John Knox contended for a thoroughly presbyterian form of church government—giving a body of elders authority over a local congregation.

The next century or so witnessed further tensions among the ranks of those who had been influenced by the Reformation. The first great rift in the church in England came when a royal proclamation demanded complete conformity to the settled order of the Church of England on the part of all and acknowledgement of the King's supremacy. Some 1,500 clergymen refused to conform. These so-called 'separatists' rejected the principle of a national church, favouring the system of church government first known as 'Independency' and later as 'Congregationalism'. They contended that each congregation should be autonomous and governed by its own members.

It was early in the seventeenth century that the Baptists emerged as a distinct body. They objected to infant baptism, maintaining that baptism should be by total immersion and should be only for those who professed a personal faith in Christ. In time the Baptists themselves became divided into different groups—General Baptists who believed Christ died for all men and Particular Baptists who held that he died only for the elect.

The Society of Friends—Quakers—was another Protestant group that came into being in the seventeenth century. Their stand lay upon the 'priesthood of all believers' and the importance of the 'inner light' whereby people were encouraged to wait for the Spirit to speak in and through them. They rejected the idea of ordained clergy.

The eighteenth century witnessed the evangelical revival, the importance of which cannot be exaggerated. Once more the basic doctrines of the gospel were freely preached. Nevertheless, this occasioned further fragmentation in the church. The leaders of the revival were, for the most part, loyal Anglicans and they certainly did not set out to found a new denomination. However, the 'old wineskins' could not contain the 'new wine' and, as an outcome of the revival, Methodism was born. John Wesley had spearheaded the Revival but within six years of his death the first secession within Methodism took place when the Methodist New Connexion was formed. Over the years there were further secessions. The cause of the divisions was usually over the issue of church government rather than over doctrine. In 1932 the three largest groups of Methodists, the Wesleyan, Primitive and United Methodists, came together to form the Methodist Church. The Methodist New Connexion, together with the Bible Christians, had joined together earlier, in 1907, to form the United Methodist Church.

In 1827 the group known as the Christian Brethren came into being. Though originating in Dublin, their first congregation was formed in Plymouth, hence the name 'Plymouth Brethren'. It was never intended to be a new denomination but, to quote one of its founders, Anthony Norris Groves, its aim was that 'men should come together in all simplicity as disciples, not waiting on any pulpit or ministry, but trusting that the Lord will edify us together by ministering to us, as he sees good, from ourselves'. Sadly, it was not long before the Brethren themselves became divided into 'Open' and 'Exclusive' sections.

In 1865 William Booth founded the 'Christian Mission' in East London, and it took the name 'Salvation Army' some thirteen years later. It was essentially an evangelistic movement and it was not originally intended that it should become a denomination, although that is now the position.

The early years of the twentieth century saw the emergence of the Pentecostal movement. Like the Salvation Army, early Pentecostalists did not intend to form a new denomination but rather to emphasize biblical truths that they believed had been neglected. In fact, several new denominations were spawned by the Pentecostal movement including the Assemblies of God, the Elim Church, the Apostolic Church and the Church of God in Christ. In more recent years we have seen the spread of Pentecostal or charismatic teaching in many branches of the Christian church, but this in turn has frequently been followed by splits and divisions and the spread of the house-church movement.

In the very sketchy outline of church history that we have attempted, enough has been said to emphasize the fact of our 'unhappy divisions'. It seems Christians simply cannot stay together for long. The issues that have historically caused division would seem mostly to hinge on doctrinal differences, and varying ideas on church government. Nevertheless, it has to be admitted that sometimes division has been the result of personality clashes between Christian leaders.

In the light of our Lord's prayer in the Upper Room, the history of the Christian church makes sad reading.

As we suggested at the beginning of this chapter the multiplicity of denominations is particularly confusing to those who become Christians without any denominational background and who seek to join a local church. Increasingly, the tendency is for such people to gravitate towards a warm fellowship where the gospel as they understand it is faithfully preached. The denominational 'label' becomes very much a secondary consideration. In some circles the very word 'denomination' has become a dirty word and there are even churches that choose to be known as 'undenominational'. This, however, is hardly a solution to the problem since in time so-called 'undenominational' churches do in fact become a new denomination!

5

Ecumenical Endeavours

The Greek word *oikoumene* from which 'ecumenical' derives, meant simply the whole inhabited earth. In its earliest usage it described that part of the world that had come under the influence of Greek civilization as opposed to barbarian lands. Then, with the rise of Rome, the Greeks acknowledged the Romans as masters of the *oikoumene*. It is also a New Testament word (Acts 7:6; Mt 24:14; Heb 2:5). At an early stage in Christian history when a word was needed to express the range of the church's fellowship, this was the word chosen. Thus there were a number of 'ecumenical' councils, the first of which was held at Nicaea in 325. To these councils came bishops and other leaders from all over the Christian world.

Every generation of Christians has produced men and women of vision who have sought to demonstrate the oneness of believers in Christ. The Puritan, Richard Baxter (1615–91), for example, tried to ignore differences over church government between Presbyterians, Episcopalians and Independents, and secured in Kidderminster a large degree of co-operation in pastoral work among the local ministers. William Carey, the 'father of modern missions', proposed in 1806 that there should be 'a meeting of all denominations of Christians at the Cape of Good Hope somewhere about 1810', to be followed by a similar gathering once every ten years. Carey made this suggestion in a letter to his friend Andrew Fuller, secretary of the newly-formed Baptist Missionary Society, but Fuller was not so enthusiastic. 'I consider this as one of brother Carey's pleasing dreams', he wrote.

From Carey's day onwards in India, Japan, China and Latin America, regular gatherings of missionaries of various nationalities and denominations were held. At the same time, various moves were made in England to bring together like-minded Christians of different denominations, the most significant of which was the gathering in 1795 of a group of Anglicans, Presbyterians, Methodists and Independents, which led to the formation of the London Missionary Society. At the inaugural meeting an Anglican declared that 'the petty distinctions among us of names and forms, the diversities of administrations and modes of Church order, we agree, shall this day be merged in the greater, nobler and characteristic name of Christians'. In 1819, in London, a group of secretaries of different missionary societies, Anglican and Free Church, met for 'mutual counsel and fellowship'. This group continued to meet until comparatively recently, and was known as the 'London Secretaries' Association'.

In 1842 a German Pastor, T. F. Knieval, toured England, France, Belgium and Switzerland, pleading for an organization that would constitute 'a spiritual union amongst all those in all lands who are fighting for God's Holy Cause and for the pure Gospel'. The same year, at a meeting of the Congregational Union in London, John Angell James urged the formation of an Evangelical Union of Protestants, while similar pleas were being voiced in Scotland by such men as Thomas Chalmers.

Largely as an outcome of these endeavours, the Evangelical Alliance was formed in London in 1846. Some 800 delegates from more than fifty denominations and many different countries attended the inaugural meeting at which a motion was passed declaring that they had met 'not to create Christian union but to confess the unity which the Church of Christ possessed as His body'. In moving the resolution, Dr Wardlaw expressed his belief, which was evidently that of the Assembly, that 'when a sinner accepted Christ as his Saviour he became a member of the Lord's body, and became at the same moment one with all who were of Christ throughout the earth'.

On the third day of the conference the doctrinal basis of the Alliance was decided upon, and it was stated that 'The parties composing the Alliance shall be such persons only as hold and maintain what is usually understood to be evangelical views in regard to certain stated matters of doctrine'.

Before the Conference broke up, consideration was given as to what the Alliance should do. It was generally agreed that its great object was to be the promotion of Christian unity and that its members should do all in their power to further this object. So-called 'practical resolutions' were then passed, and in later years these were read and emphasized at every subsequent General Conference of the Alliance.

In the succeeding years many branches of the Evangelical Alliance were formed in different countries. The unifying factor between the various branches of the alliance became the common observance of a Universal Week of Prayer, during the first full week of January. Within the ranks of the Alliance in these formative years the word 'ecumenical' was frequently used to denote that it transcended national and denominational barriers. As Dr Norman Goodall has pointed out, the terms 'evangelical' and 'ecumenical' were accepted as belonging together in those days! The use of the word 'ecumenical' did not arouse suspicion in evangelical circles.

There were a number of other societies formed that also transcended denominational barriers, among them the British and Foreign Bible Society (1804), with a Committee composed equally of Anglicans and non-conformists. Earlier, in 1799, the Religious Tract Society, later to become the United Society for Christian Literature, had come into being, and this also worked through and for different Protestant denominations. Other 'ecumenical' organizations that emerged in the nineteenth century included the YMCA and the YWCA.

William Carey's dream of a worldwide gathering of Christian leaders, interdenominational in its scope and missionary in its purpose, was to be realized in 1910 when a World Missionary Conference was convened in Edinburgh. A somewhat similar conference had been held in New York in 1900, known as an Ecumenical Missionary Conference. Among those present, as Chairman of the Youth Committee at the New York Conference, was John R. Mott, destined to become one of the leading lay figures in the early history of the ecumenical movement. He was also one of the architects of the YMCA movement, and founder in 1895 of the World's Student Christian Federation. He lived to become the first Honorary President of the World Council of Churches. President Woodrow Wilson described him as 'the world's most useful man', and over the years honours were lavished upon him by one country after another. This American Methodist layman was Chairman of the World Missionary Conference in Edinburgh in 1910.

The Conference at Edinburgh was more representative and better organized than any previous conference of this kind, and among the 1,200 delegates were representatives from Asia and Africa. The Conference made provision for the continuance of its work by the formation of a Continuation Committee. At Edinburgh it had been generally agreed that orthodox Christian doctrine was essential to any effective programme of worldwide missionary co-operation. The Conference called for 'the evangelisation of the world in our generation'. There was basic agreement on the missionary motive, method and objective.

As a direct outcome of Edinburgh 1910, two types of agencies developed—national conferences of missionary societies, and national councils in which churches and missions co-operated for common action. A little more than a decade after its formation the Edinburgh Continuation Committee changed its name and became known as the International Missionary Council.

Seventeen national organizations linked up with the Council when it was formed in 1921. These were predominantly Missionary Councils and National Federation of Missionary Societies. Thirteen out of the seventeen were from the so-called 'sending' countries, the remaining four were in Asia or the Middle East.

Following its formation in 1921, the International Missionary Council held a series of World Conferences. At the Conference in Jerusalem in 1928 there were clear indications of a changing emphasis—non-Christian religions were recognized as collaborators in a common battle against materialism and secularism. There were growing tensions between Bible-believing Christians and those with a more 'liberal' attitude to Scripture, leading to splits in some missionary societies that in turn resulted in a number of new independent missions coming into being.

There were other streams that flowed in the direction of the ecumenical movement. A notable gathering was held in Great Britain in 1924 entitled 'Conference on Christian Politics, Economics and Citizenship' (COPEC). This Conference met under the chairmanship of Archbishop William Temple.

In 1925 the Universal Christian Conference on Life and Work met in Stockholm under the chairmanship of Nathan Söderblom, Archbishop of Uppsala. Among those present were representatives of the Orthodox Church. The declared purpose of this Conference was 'To concentrate the mind of Christendom on the mind of Christ as revealed in the Gospels towards those great social, industrial and international questions which are so acutely urgent in our civilization'. The emphasis was upon the social implications of the gospel. The contention was that, while 'doctrine separates, service unites'.

A more permanent organization known as the Universal Christian Council for Life and Work was later set up, the declared objective of which was 'to perpetuate and strengthen the fellowship between the Churches in the application of Christian ethics to social problems in modern life'. A parallel council known as the World Council on Faith and Order came into being in 1927.

The Edinburgh Conference of 1910 had not, generally speaking, been concerned with doctrinal issues, nor had it dealt with matters pertaining to the ministry and sacraments or the ordering of the life of the church. It was recognized that questions of this kind could only be responsibly discussed by accredited representatives and theologians of the churches themselves. The Faith and Order movement existed as an independent body until the launching of the World Council of Churches (WCC) in 1948.

Representatives both of the Life and Work movement and the Faith and Order movement met in separate conferences in 1937. Before the meetings of these two movements had closed each of them passed a resolution favouring the creation of a Council of Churches. The name World Council of Churches was suggested by Dr S. M. Cavert, then General Secretary of the Federal Council of Churches in America. A provisional committee was set up in 1937 that took the responsibility of shaping the council-to-be during a period in which it became known as 'the World Council of Churches in process of formation'. The first chairman of the provisional committee was Archbishop William Temple.

During the war years meetings of the provisional committee were impossible, although ways and means were found for keeping its members in touch with one another. It had originally been intended that the first Assembly of the World Council should be held in 1941. In February 1947 a conference was held at Geneva when final steps were taken with a view to the calling of a General Assembly at Amsterdam in 1948.

The Council took formal shape at a memorable gathering in Amsterdam and the veteran layman John R. Mott was appointed Honorary President. Some 147 churches became members of the Council at its inaugural assembly, giving assent to the 'Amsterdam Message', and affirming 'here at Amsterdam we have committed ourselves afresh to Him and have covenanted with one another in constituting the World Council of Churches. We intend to stay together'. The original basis of the Council, adopted at Amsterdam, was as follows: 'The World Council of Churches is a fellowship of Churches which accept our Lord Jesus Christ as God and Saviour'. In 1962 this basis was expanded to read thus: 'The World Council of Churches is a fellowship of Churches which confess the Lord Jesus Christ as God and Saviour according to the Scriptures, and therefore seek to fulfil together their common calling to the glory of the one God, Father, Son and Holy Spirit'.

In 1962, when the World Council met in conference at New Delhi, the integration of the World Council with the International Missionary Council (IMC) took place. The IMC became the Commission of World Mission and Evangelism of the World Council.

Broadly speaking, the formation of the World Council of Churches met with a threefold reaction:

1. Widespread approval from many of the larger non-

Roman churches and denominations.

2. 'Benevolent neutrality' from some Protestant denominations, not prepared for various reasons to apply for membership.
3. Determined opposition from certain strongly 'fundamentalist' groups that joined together to form in Amsterdam in 1948 the International Council of Christian Churches under the leadership of Dr Carl McIntyre. (Roman Catholics stood aside from the World Council initially.)

Many evangelical Christians have been from the outset critical of certain aspects of and trends in the ecumenical movement, although many have recognized that relationship or otherwise to the World Council of Churches should not be made the test of fellowship. Evangelicals adopting this more tolerant position have tended to find their rally point in national Evangelical Fellowships and Alliances, and at the world level in the World Evangelical Fellowship.

The main criticisms levelled against the ecumenical movement have been that it tends in the direction of a 'superchurch', it is prepared to buy unity at the expense of truth; it seeks rapprochement with the Roman Catholic Church; it is 'inclusivist' in its membership and, some would say, it is a major distraction from the real need of the church for spiritual renewal. Certainly, its concept of unity could be said to be organizational and bureaucratic rather than essentially spiritual.

The emergence of the ecumenical movement has precipitated something of a crisis among evangelicals. A number of factors have contributed to this, including the call issued by Dr Martyn Lloyd-Jones when speaking at the National Assembly of Evangelicals in 1966 to evangelicals to come out of their 'mixed' denominations. Another factor was the Keele Congress of Anglican evangelicals that made it clear that official evangelical Anglican policy was to remain within the ecumenical framework, and to bear a witness within a comprehensive church rather than separate from it. The result of all this has been a hardening of certain 'party' lines. The Evangelical Alliance in particular has come under fire from the 'separatists' in the evangelical camp for its allegedly soft line with regard to the ecumenical movement. The separatists have found their rallying point in the British Evangelical Council which has been in existence for several years, but has only really come into its own comparatively recently. The British Evangelical Council makes no secret of its attitude towards the World Council of Churches, and believes that it is incumbent on all true evangelicals to take an equally strong line.

The present situation is distressing in many ways, and one can but pray that Bible-believing Christians may learn increasingly how to speak the truth in love. The real point at issue in the current debate concerns the nature of the church itself. Those who are content to remain in the ecumenical movement are usually content also to remain in a comprehensive church, while, generally speaking, the 'separatists' are those whose quest is a 'pure' church made up exclusively of 'born again' believers. I have personal sympathies with such an ideal, although the history of the church would suggest it is unattainable on earth, and that those who have been over-zealous in pursuing it have sometimes caused more division than they could possibly have anticipated. The quest for visible unity must and will go on, but unity like charity begins 'at home' and our first and foremost task is to preserve unity within the local church.

6

The Meal that Unites?

It should be a matter of deep concern that not all Christians feel able to sit down with fellow believers at the Lord's table. The late Archbishop Temple described this situation as being 'the greatest of all scandals on the face of the world'.

Christians of varying traditions may worship together, pray together, and go out into the streets to bear witness unitedly, but when it comes to partaking of Holy Communion they go their separate ways. Yet, is it not true that one of the basic truths that we express at the Lord's table is the fact that we are united in our mutual dependence upon the saviourhood of Jesus Christ?

There have been, of course, occasions when Christians of different traditions have broken through denominational barriers and have, in fact, held united communion services. Such services have been held in a number of localities and one is held, and has been for many years, at the conclusion of the Keswick Convention. Similar united communion services have taken place at the Royal Albert Hall. While these services have the support of many Christians in different sections of the Christian church, there are others who feel that these occasions in fact retard the process of re-union. They feel that at such services the real issues that divide Christians are not faced as they should be.

Our approach to this whole subject is inevitably coloured by our own background. Those who have been brought up in the Free Churches are accustomed to an invitation that is given to all who sincerely love Christ to meet at the Lord's table. In General Baptist churches, Presbyterian churches, Methodist churches and, of course, in the Church of Scotland this is the recognized practice. Those who take up the position of inter-communion believe that it is the Lord's table and, as such, is open to all believers. The onus is placed upon the individual, 'let a man examine himself'. If a man feels in his own heart free to come to the Lord's table because he sincerely believes in Jesus then the church authorities do not feel that it is right to refuse this.

Increasingly, it is also the practice in many Anglican churches to welcome to the Lord's table those who, while not being members of the Church of England, are nevertheless communicant members of their own churches.

We sometimes overlook the fact that Holy Communion is the Lord's Supper and not the private rite of a particular denomination. In an article some years ago on the subject of inter-communion, John Stott asked the question:

> God does not insist on episcopal confirmation before He accepts sinners into fellowship with Himself: so, why should we insist upon it before we receive them into fellowship with us? Are we more exclusive than God? Are we spiritual segregationalists separating ourselves

> and practising a kind of ecclesiastical apartheid with no Biblical warrant? Peter had to learn that lack of Mosaic circumcision was no barrier to communion. We need to learn that lack of episcopal confirmation is no barrier either.

John Stott went on to point out that in various sections of the Christian church this false spirit of exclusiveness manifests itself with the result that men create their own conditions of fellowship. God, on the other hand, imposes no such conditions. The only condition he lays down is justification by faith.

This is not an argument against church discipline, for every branch of the Christian church has a perfect right to make its own rules for its own members. In the Church of England, for example, confirmation is the means whereby men and women enter into full church membership. Is there any valid scriptural reason, however, why this rule should be imposed on valid members of other churches who have entered into full membership of their own particular branch of the Christian church? Those who share John Stott's point of view interpret confirmation as being a domestic issue relating to the Church of England itself. He argues that there is ample historic evidence from the principles and practice of the English reformers and their successors that baptized communicant members of other reformed churches should be allowed to visit Church of England churches and partake of Holy Communion in them.

No one would argue for communicant members of other branches of the Christian church regularly partaking of Holy Communion in the Church of England.

Obviously if they wish to do this they should consider being confirmed and thus becoming full members of that church. As visitors, however, surely they have a right to expect hospitality at the Lord's table. John Stott believes that inter-communion has a clear biblical warrant. I quote again from his article:

> If the practice of an open table is denied, it is not custom only which is violated but the truth of the Gospel. To deny a fellow Christian, a believing baptized communicant member of his own church, occasional access to the Lord's table in the Church of England simply because he has not been episcopally confirmed, is an offence to the God who has justified him, and an insult to a brother for whom Christ died. Am I to regard a justified fellow believer as unclean that I withdraw from him? I seem to hear again the heavenly voice which spoke to Peter—'What God has cleansed you must not call common'.

One recognizes, of course, that this issue is not as simple as sometimes portrayed. We are not only concerned with the admission or otherwise of non-conformists to the Lord's table as occasional visitors in an Anglican church. Inter-communion implies reciprocal communion. Free churchmen realize that, for Anglicans, this does involve them in very serious issues. It does, in effect, cause them to rethink their position in relation to the question of the validity of non-episcopal ministries and sacraments. To believe in inter-communion does imply acceptance of the validity of non-episcopal ministries as being real and efficacious ministries within the body of Christ.

Anglo-Catholics in the Church of England have

made their position abundantly clear. They maintain that anyone administering the sacrament of Holy Communion must be a priest episcopally ordained. For that reason of course the Church of South India is not recognized. Obviously there is a real divergence of opinion here. Evangelical Christians generally reject any such rigid mechanical and exclusive view of the ministry that would appear to them to be contrary to the whole tenor of the Christian gospel and teaching of Jesus.

We cannot accept any doctrine that assumes the exclusive priesthood of episcopally ordained ministers. While we may recognize the fact of episcopacy we do not agree that episcopacy is one of the essential marks of the church. Indeed the Church of England, though an episcopal church, does not make any such claim in its Articles of Religion. In Article 19, for example, where the visible church is defined as 'a congregation of faithful men in the which the pure Word of God is preached, and the Sacraments be duly administered according to Christ's ordinance', there is no mention of any particular form of ministry as being essential to a true church. As Canon Frank Colquhoun has pointed out, 'If apostolic succession through an unbroken chain of Bishops is really a matter of such vital importance, it is inconceivable that the Article should make no attempt either to define or to defend the doctrine'.

Thus, among those who are basically in agreement with regard to the main tenets of their faith, coming together at the Lord's table presents no difficulties. Matters of church government are questions upon which we agree to differ; our oneness is found in our relationship to Christ, the Head of the church. To many of us the doctrine of justification by faith alone is at the very heart of the gospel, and we must resolutely resist any teaching that conflicts with the sufficiency of God's grace for man's salvation, and introduces in any form the idea of human merit. Salvation is not something man achieves for himself, or earns; it is the gift of God's grace to be accepted through simple trust in Jesus Christ as Saviour and Lord. The work, the sacrifice, the merit, the glory, are all his, not ours. From first to last salvation is of the Lord. On our part nothing is required but faith. We put our trust in what he has done for us, not in anything that we have done for him. We are bound, on scriptural grounds, to reject anything that denies or tends to obscure the once-for-all-ness of Christ's one great sacrifice for sin. Our stress is upon the fact that he made a full, perfect, and sufficient sacrifice for the sins of the whole world, bearing our judgement; purchasing our salvation. This atoning work can never be repeated, nor can we add anything to it. This we believe is the soul-liberating truth that is at the very heart of Paul's theology and that was rediscovered so gloriously at the time of the Reformation in the sixteenth century.

Those of us who find ourselves as one in such matters as these feel that it is perfectly logical to meet at that place where we look back in adoring wonder to the cross, and worship him who loved us and gave himself for us. At the cross we do not contend with one another regarding episcopal or non-episcopal ministries. The merits lie not in those who administer the sacrament but in the One whose body and blood is symbolized by the bread and the wine.

The Reverend John Goss, himself an Anglican

minister, pointed out in an article on church unity and inter-communion:

> In seeking complete union it is fatally easy to overlook the unity already given to all believers and to neglect the natural means of its manifestation through the fellowship of the Lord's table. I believe more and more Christian men and women are feeling this way and I also believe it is something the Spirit is saying to the churches. Surely unity in faith rather than unity in order is the pre-requisite of Christian fellowship? I believe there are many loyal Anglicans who do not hold to the position that the Sacrament is only valid if received at the hands of an episcopally-ordained clergyman.

Christ and his disciples clearly regarded the Lord's Supper as, among other things, a symbol and foretaste of the unity that will yet find full expression in the age to come. It is tragic therefore that Christians still allow differences of interpretation regarding the significance of this sacred meal to divide them, and that many still refuse to recognize the validity of others' celebrations.

7

Together in Evangelism

The 'great commission' was given by Jesus to the whole church and Christians from all branches of it at least pay lip-service to that fact. It would seem, therefore, that here is an obvious area where we ought to be able to do things together. Of course, there must be common agreement as to *what* constitutes the gospel that is to be preached—and sadly, not all Christians are of one mind on this issue. As long ago as 1918 the Archbishops published a report in which they attempted to define what is meant by evangelism: 'To evangelize is so to present Christ Jesus in the power of the Holy Spirit that men shall come to put their trust in God through him, to accept him as their Saviour, and serve him as their King in the fellowship of his church'. That may sound a rather wordy definition—to put it more simply, evangelism involves the proclamation to sinful men and women of Jesus Christ as Saviour and Lord. It involves the delivery of a particular message the response to which should be 'repentance towards God' and 'faith in our Lord Jesus Christ'. Canon Douglas Webster has made the significant observation that 'the more vague Christians allow themselves to be about the basic truths of the faith, the more indifferent they appear to grow about their obligation in respect of mission'.

A group of churches in a locality that are in basic agreement regarding the content of the gospel message may decide to join together in a united evangelistic campaign. Such an effort is sometimes spoken of as city-wide or mass evangelism. It is a concentration of spiritual effort in a given place for a limited time, with the aim of presenting the gospel to as large a segment of the community as possible.

Public meetings are arranged, often on neutral ground, with the goal of attracting the non-churchgoer. Usually there is a lot of music—choir and solo items, choruses, rousing hymns— and testimonies. Following the address an appeal is made for commitment to Christ, followed by an after-meeting or a time of personal counselling for those inquirers who have responded to the invitation. United evangelism of this kind presupposes the services of an evangelist, or team of evangelists, coming at the invitation of the local community.

Mass evangelism is an exceedingly ancient method of conveying God's message to men. Long before the advent of modern technology providing landline relays, video-tapes and closed-circuit television, vast crowds have gathered at different periods in history to hear evangelists proclaim the good news of salvation.

Jonathan Edwards preached to great crowds in New England in the eighteenth century in spite of fierce criticism from many church leaders.

George Whitefield, in the eighteenth century, embarked on a lifetime of evangelism in Britain and America. In New England alone, out of a population of 300,000, an estimated 50,000 professed faith in Christ.

John Wesley (1703–91) set out as an open-air preacher in April 1739 and at the age of 86 addressed an audience of 25,000. During his lifetime he probably led as many as 180,000 people to Christ. He regularly travelled 4,500 miles a year, mostly on horseback, preaching two or three times a day.

Charles Finney (1792–1875) was an American evangelist of great ability. He visited England on several occasions and was the first of the great evangelists to ask people to 'come forward' at his meetings. In 1832 the Presbyterian churches in America alone received 34,000 new members as a result of Finney's missions.

Dwight L. Moody, with his musical accompanist *Ira Sankey*, had a remarkable ministry on both sides of the Atlantic during the nineteenth century. The two men came to England for the first time in 1873 with astonishing results.

R. A. Torrey, Charles D. Alexander and later *Chapman* and *Alexander* conducted large-scale evangelistic campaigns in the early years of the present century, while *Billy Sunday's* campaigns reached their zenith in the decade 1910–20.

Billy Graham's first city-wide crusade was in Los Angeles in 1949 and his first large crusade in Britain was at Harringay in 1954–55. Since then he has conducted a number of large-scale crusades in the British Isles.

More recently, the South American evangelist, *Luis Palau*, has been here to conduct city-wide missions.

A number of other men between the two world wars and subsequently have exercised a powerful ministry in this kind of evangelism, including Lionel B. Fletcher,

William P. Nicholson, the brothers Wood, Stephen and George Jeffreys, Lindsay Glegg, Tom Rees, Eric Hutchings, Don Summers and Dick Saunders.

Of course, we could go much further back than the eighteenth century to find examples of large-scale evangelism. Great reformers such as Latimer and Ridley drew great crowds in the sixteenth century. John Wycliffe—'the Morning Star of the Reformation'—and his followers made a profound impact in the fourteenth century. But we can even go back to the New Testament itself. What of Paul on Mars Hill or Peter on the day of Pentecost? Clearly these men spoke to large gatherings and no one would deny the effectiveness of such occasions, nor question the fact that the preachers called for a verdict. Jesus himself addressed crowds numbering thousands, while John the Baptist's preaching also drew great multitudes.

There are some distinct advantages in co-operative evangelism, not the least of which is that it demonstrates spiritual unity in action. Churches working together are more likely to make an effective impact on the community at large and perhaps attract the interest of the mass media. This form of evangelism involves the recruitment, training and deployment of many different Christian workers from a variety of denominational backgrounds. It also provides, of course, an opportunity for a gifted evangelist to be used to maximum effect.

Paul made clear his policy—'By all possible means I might save some' (1 Cor 9:22). United or mass evangelism is *one* means which, under God, has been used to save men and women. Its appeal may largely be to those who already have some loose connection with the church, or who have been brought along to meetings by church members, but it should not be rejected on that account.

But there are also some problems. The limits of co-operation have to be decided upon. There must be basic agreement as to the content of the message as well as acceptance of the validity of the methods used. The danger of undue emotionalism is very real when large crowds gather. The referral of inquirers is another area that poses problems in a united campaign. To which churches shall those who profess conversion be directed? What if some claim at least a nominal link with a church that lacks vitality and would appear quite incapable of nurturing newborn 'babes in Christ'? In Luis Palau's Mission to London in 1984 it was agreed that those professing conversion not having any previous church connections would only be referred to churches having established nurture groups to look after them.

It is sometimes levelled against this form of evangelism that it is an affront to the sovereignty of God in salvation and an attempt to pressurize men and women unduly. The complaint is also made that it is a distraction from the work of the local churches and of individual Christians who carry the primary responsibility for the work of evangelism.

Undoubtedly, there are justifiable criticisms of mass evangelism that have to be heeded. There is always the danger of relying too heavily on the evangelist's persuasive personality or failing to declare the whole counsel of God in order to make the message more palatable. Furthermore, the temptation to rely upon techniques rather than upon the work of the Holy

Spirit must be studiously avoided. It would be better for those who come forward at such missions to be referred to as 'inquirers' rather than 'converts'. Time alone will prove whether or not their response was real rather than superficial.

Despite these problems, one of the great benefits of co-operative evangelism undoubtedly lies in the deepening sense of fellowship experienced in the local Christian community irrespective of denominational differences, to say nothing of its demonstration to the pagan world of the essential unity of believers (Jn 17:20–21). The matter of 'the appeal' will no doubt remain a thorny question. Large evangelistic missions do sometimes produce a crop of spurious conversions, especially when the appeal has been mainly, if not entirely, directed towards the emotions. Deliberate psychological pressure is inexcusable. Conversion is the work of the Holy Spirit and of him alone. On the other hand a public witness to a commitment to Christ is often of great spiritual benefit to the person concerned. Furthermore, it enables the convert or inquirer to receive immediate counsel from a trained Christian worker. The debate will long continue regarding the validity or otherwise of the invitation system. The fact remains that God has blessed, and no doubt will continue to bless, large-scale evangelistic campaigns, but those responsible for them must always be sure to see that their reliance is not on men or methods, wide publicity or efficient organization, but on the living God. It should also be noted that very often churches that have co-operated in supporting a large-scale local evangelistic mission tend to grow together and find themselves working together on other projects when the campaign is over. United evangelistic campaigns undoubtedly create a sense of togetherness among Christians in any given locality. Quite apart from the mission itself, untold benefits arise from participation in the training classes that are held beforehand which are organized on an interdenominational basis.

8

'In All Things Charity'

The dictum 'In necessary things unity; in doubtful things liberty; in all things charity' is attributed to Richard Baxter. It is a saying much beloved by those Christians who are concerned with the subject of spiritual unity. The point at issue of course concerns what things we are to regard as 'necessary'. Most Christian bodies have some kind of basis of faith in which they set forth those doctrines that they believe to be fundamental, but they differ somewhat in the actual phraseology used. Broadly speaking, however, it would be true to say that in almost every statement there is a reference to the divine inspiration and supreme and final authority of the Scriptures, the deity of our Lord Jesus Christ, the finished sacrifice of the cross as the one all-sufficient atonement for sin, the fact of salvation by grace through faith in our Lord Jesus Christ and not through our own works or merits, the regenerating and sanctifying work of the Holy Spirit, and the personal return of Christ. Such basic truths would certainly be considered by any evangelical organization to be 'necessary things' since we hold that, if there is to be any effective co-operation, there must be basic agreement on such truths. We cannot enjoy a sense of unity with those who worship a different God or believe in a different Christ, or preach a different gospel.

It is possibly the second phrase in Baxter's dictum that causes most concern. What exactly are the things that may be described as 'doubtful'? Where are we to draw the line? Most would agree that such matters as church order, forms of worship, and systems of government are questions on which there need not be unanimity. Differences on these points need not be barriers to the enjoyment of spiritual unity. Our many interdenominational societies, and such movements as the Keswick Convention, all bear witness to the fact that there is an underlying spiritual unity that crosses denominational barriers. Episcopalians and Free Churchmen, members of the Christian Brethren and Salvationists, can enjoy deep fellowship in the things of God, and yet differ greatly on such matters as we have outlined. There are, however, a number of issues that do tend to divide our ranks.

One such issue concerns our attitude towards the ecumenical movement itself. This has probably been the most debated question of all in evangelical circles in recent years. There are those who take the extreme position of withdrawing fellowship from any Christian, however evangelical he himself may be, if he happens to be linked with a denomination that in turn is in association with the World Council of Churches. The unhappy phrase 'guilt by association' is sometimes used in such a situation. In some cases this issue of separation is actually separating evangelicals from one another. Whereas there must be few, if any, Bible-believing Christians who do not have misgivings regarding the ecumenical movement, particularly because of its wide embracing inclusivism, we must recognize the fact that there are those who genuinely feel called to bear their testimony from within its ranks. Can we justifiably, before God, withhold our fellowship from such brethren? A basic principle written into the Constitution of the World Evangelical Fellowship, and also into that of the Evangelical Missionary Alliance, is that 'members shall not be the subject of criticism or censure because of any other associations, national or international, in which they are involved'. It is held that such relationships shall be deemed to be the private concern of individual members.

There are also doctrinal issues that tend to divide our ranks, for example tension exists between those often described as 'hyper-Calvinists' and those who would be loosely termed 'Arminians'. The issue here is largely one of emphasis. Any reader of the Scriptures is bound to recognize the fact that the Bible clearly teaches divine sovereignty and election, but he is equally bound to face the fact of human responsibility and accountability as being scriptural concepts. Because of our human frailty we tend to lose our sense of balance. The result is that you sometimes meet those whose emphasis upon election and predestination is so strong that it almost amounts to fatalism, with the result that their interest in and concern for evangelism is largely negated. On the other hand, there are those who seem to suggest that if only we employ the right techniques in evangelism, we can more or less guarantee results. In Scripture we do not find that belief in divine sovereignty and human free will are mutually exclusive—indeed, they are held together in tension. Let Calvinists and Arminians pray together and seek the mind of the Spirit together, rather than engage in 'in-fighting' that can only weaken the cause of Christ as we face a common enemy.

Another doctrinal issue that has been allowed, in some cases, to divide Bible-believing Christians from one another concerns prophecy. There are different schools of thought regarding the chronological order of events in connection with the second advent of Christ, and particularly the millennium. Broadly speaking, there are three main views, usually labelled pre-millennial, post-millennial and a-millennial.

The pre-millennialist believes in a literal millennium lasting a thousand years (Rev 20:1–10) but holds that the Lord will return before the millennium. Post-millennialists take the view that Christ will return after the millennium which has been described as the 'golden age' of the church. A-millennialists hold that there is no sufficient ground in Scripture for the expectation of a millennium in the sense of a literal thousand-year period of time. Some teach that the millennium symbolizes the joy of Christian experience in this present age. The figure of a thousand is seen as symbolic of the idea of fullness and completeness.

While it would probably be true that the post-millennial view has on the whole commended itself more especially to those with 'liberal' tendencies, certainly the a-millenial view and the pre-millennial view are both held by evangelical Christians. We recognize, of course, that the pre-millennial view takes many different forms, including that usually known as 'dispensationalism' which claims that God has dealt differently with men during different eras of biblical history. This is not the place to go into great detail in relation to these matters but, since our concern here relates to *future* events, surely there must be liberty in the matter of interpretation? Have we any right to bind one another to a particular viewpoint in regard to prophetic events? Of course we must insist on belief in the personal return of Christ—that is a fundamental tenet of the Christian faith if the New Testament is to be our guide at all. By all means let us study the different theories and interpretations related to Christ's return, and let us seek to come to our own conclusions in these matters, but, having done so, surely we should be sufficiently charitable to recognize that there are other possible lines of thought.

Yet another issue that arises in evangelical circles at the present time concerns the doctrine of the Holy Spirit. No Bible-believing Christian finds any difficulty in confessing belief in the personality of the Holy Spirit and in his regenerating and sanctifying work in the life of the believer. There is, however, a considerable divergence of opinion on just what is meant by such phrases as the baptism of the Spirit, the filling of the Spirit, and the nature of spiritual gifts. It is perhaps particularly encouraging that at the present time so many Christians are applying themselves to the detailed study of the biblical doctrine of the Holy Spirit; one suspects, however, that difficulties of interpretation will still remain. Scripture is not always as explicit as some would suggest—it may be that here, too, we have got to agree to differ with some of our brethren, and yet not withhold fellowship from them. Gone are the days, we hope, when Christians wrote booklets dismissing the whole of pentecostal teaching as 'a delusion of the devil'. From the charismatic side we may hope, also, that there will be increasing charity, so that fellow Christians who may not have travelled by precisely the same pathway, may nevertheless be recognized as being as much in earnest for the deepening of spiritual life as their brethren in the charismatic movement even though they may not describe their experience in quite the same terms.

Baptism is another bone of contention, but even this, important an issue as it is, should not be allowed to divide Christians from co-operation with one another. While some feel there is a clear-cut case for believers' baptism—and that alone—in the New Testament, others with equal sincerity feel that the children of believing parents may be baptized and brought into covenant relationship with the Lord, much in the same way as were the Israelite children through the rite of circumcision. It may be that here, too, the Scriptures do not make the issue as explicit as some tend to suggest. Of course, there are also differences among Christians regarding the mode of baptism, even when they may be agreed that it should be reserved for believers. While some insist on total immersion, believing this to be the New Testament practice, others argue for the use of a token amount of water, just as in the Lord's Supper a token amount of wine and bread is used.

We may well ask how it is that those with a common faith who, with equal sincerity, accept the Bible as the fully inspired word of God and authoritative in all matters of faith and practice, can in fact come to different conclusions regarding such issues as we have mentioned? The answer surely must be that the Scriptures themselves are not dogmatic on these issues.

They leave a certain amount of room for differences of interpretation, and, if this is so, we must be prepared to do the same. 'In things *necessary* unity, in *doubtful* things liberty'.

The final phrase in Richard Baxter's watchword was 'in all things *charity*'. How vitally important it is that those who are zealous for the truth should not overlook this fact. The Apostle John described Jesus as being full of grace and truth, and no doubt it is significant that these two qualities are mentioned together and in that particular order. The Apostle Paul calls upon Christians to 'speak the truth in love'. Being faithful to the word and being loving in disposition are not mutually exclusive characteristics. Rather, they should go together. All of us, and particularly those who in these days are called upon to take up some highly controversial issues, would do well to read 1 Corinthians 13 at regular intervals. We must remind ourselves of Paul's words: 'if I speak in the tongues of men and of angels, but have not love, I am only a resounding gong or a clanging cymbal. If I have the gift of prophecy and can fathom all mysteries and all knowledge, and if I have a faith that can move mountains, but have not love, I am nothing'. We need to remember that, in the last resort, the maintenance of the faith depends upon the integrity and spirituality of the people that hold it, and the manner in which it finds expression in their lives. It should be our prayer that our zeal for the truth may ever be matched by our love for the brethren, and that, as we seek to be faithful, we may be given the grace to be humble.

At a time when the subject of Christian unity is so much to the fore evangelical Christians are naturally concerned to know what are the biblical principles of co-operation. They recognize on the one hand that already they have a large measure of spiritual unity, yet at the same time they are alive to the fact that there is a great degree of unity yet to be achieved. While they have traditionally boasted of their oneness in Christ, such Christians have not in fact always expressed their unity in corporate action as much as they might have done.

It has been remarked that, at the present time, the divisions between Christians are horizontal rather than vertical. By this is meant that there are corresponding groups in the various denominations that often possess greater affinities with one another, in spite of denominational differences, than they do with some others within their own denominations! As Dr H. H. Rowdon has commented:

> The very existence of different denominations obscures the real unity which believing Christians have in Christ. It is not easy to explain why believer X attends the Methodist Church, believer Y belongs to the Baptist Church opposite and believer Z is a communicant at the Parish Church round the corner when they have more in common with one another than with many of their fellow Methodists, Baptists and Anglicans respectively. Furthermore, denominationalism stultifies Church discipline as long as persons under discipline can find a welcome elsewhere.

Christians who are of one mind regarding the fundamental truths of the gospel find themselves able to co-operate in many interdenominational activities even though they may have to agree to differ on a number of secondary issues. As has often been pointed out, the 'fellowship of the gospel' rests upon the 'faith of the gospel'.

On the other hand, there can be no effective co-operation with those who deny such basic tenets of the faith as the deity of Christ, the finished sacrifice of the cross, and the doctrine of justification by faith alone. Whereas one should be ready freely to discuss matters of Christian doctrine with those with whom one differs fundamentally, active co-operation does demand basic agreement on essential truths. Effective unity must be in the context of loyalty to the truth of the gospel.

The New Testament does, of course, give many warnings concerning false teaching. The Apostle Paul left the church at Galatia in no doubt as to what their attitude should be towards those who preached 'another gospel'. We have to be on our guard in these days of easy-going tolerance lest in the name of charity we should find ourselves 'denying the Lord that bought us'. In the second epistle of John very definite instructions are given as to correct procedure when we are confronted with those who deny the basic truths of the gospel—'If anyone comes to you and does not bring this teaching, do not take him into your house or welcome him'. It is a fact that must be faced, that in recent years a number of cults have gained favour that deny such essential doctrines as the Trinity and the deity of Christ. While most of us would hate to become 'heresy hunters', at the same time we should recognize our responsibility to 'contend for the faith' in an age when even some denominational leaders are prepared to deny basic Christian doctrines that they have pledged themselves to proclaim.

Ultimately, every man has to decide before God how far he is willing to co-operate with others who profess the name of Christ but differ on doctrinal matters. In reaching his decision he has for his guide the New Testament, and this makes it perfectly clear that the doctrine of the Person and work of Christ is of such importance that no man can agree to differ on that point. Where, therefore, the very nature of the gospel we preach is at stake there can be no possible compromise. We cannot be at one with those who believe in a different Christ and preach a different gospel and any question of active co-operation therefore is ruled out.

To sum up—Christians need to be sure of those truths that are of the very essence of the Christian faith. They need, too, to be able to distinguish such truths from matters upon which legitimately there can be differences of opinion and of interpretation. At the same time, they must recognize the necessity for acting and speaking charitably even in their dealings with those from whom they differ radically. It may be that one of the greatest needs of all is that in these days of apostacy and luke-warmness those Christians who profess to hold the apostolic faith should discover to a greater degree than ever before, ways and means whereby they themselves may co-operate more effectively in Christian work and witness.

John Calvin distinguished between those articles of faith that make up the sum of Christianity and those beliefs not sufficiently important to justify separation from other Christians. We must be careful not to attach disproportionate importance to anything not of the essence of the gospel.

Schism—the dividing of true believers over relatively

minor issues—is sinful. Often it is simply a display of carnality. Most of us have a good deal to learn about 'speaking the truth in love'. It is significant that in the pastoral epistles the man of God is reminded more than once that he is not to be a 'brawler'. We all know of churches that have been split over shibboleths, and Christian societies that have multiplied as the result of personality clashes. All of us need to pray for 'a sense of what is vital' so that while adhering tenaciously to the fundamentals of the faith, we may allow liberty to one another in matters that allow for differences of interpretation. It is tragic when Christians denounce one another in print because of differing views of prophecy or different interpretations of the doctrine of sanctification. Neither uniformity of practice nor even uniformity of belief, when it comes to secondary matters, are necessary for fellowship.

9

Unity in the Spirit?

The charismatic or renewal movement has brought a fresh dimension to the whole question of Christian unity. When the Pope visited Britain in 1982 the welcoming crowds were often heard singing choruses that one would more readily associate with the house-church movement. Prayer groups have come into being that bring together Catholics and Protestants—even in some parts of Ireland. Have the charismatics succeeded where the ecumenical bureaucrats have failed? It might be helpful to trace in broad terms the history of this remarkable movement of the Spirit.

In the late 1950s and early 1960s there were a number of groups in Britain earnestly seeking renewal. Arthur Wallis, a man with a Christian Brethren background, was one of the early leaders, as was Bryn Jones, who came from one of the Pentecostal denominations. Most of the men involved at this stage were non-conformists. They were concerned for 'whole body' ministry, and reacted strongly against institutionalism and clergy domination in the church and the idea of one-man ministry.

Meanwhile in America, the Reverend Dennis Bennett, rector of a fashionable Episcopal church, had created no small stir when he announced to his congregation that he had been 'filled with the Spirit' and spoken in other tongues just like the disciples on the Day of Pentecost. The result was that many other ministers and lay people now came forward in America to declare what God had been doing recently in their lives. In 1953 the Full Gospel Business Men's Fellowship International really got off the ground under the presidency of Demos Shakarian. Here was a lay movement emphasizing 'baptism in the Spirit' but free from the shackles of ecclesiastical sanctions. Jean Stone, a member of Dennis Bennett's church, was also baptized in the Spirit and she was to have a great influence through the magazine *Trinity*, in which she wrote.

In the early 1960s Dennis Bennett, Jean Stone and a young Lutheran pastor from California, Larry Christenson, all visited Britain and shared their 'charismatic' experiences. Slowly but surely the impact began to be felt over here. One of those who 'came into blessing' was Michael Harper, at that time a curate with the Reverend John Stott at All Souls Church, Langham Place, London. He was later to play a leading role in the Fountain Trust, which was formed in 1964 but closed down in 1980. The 1960s and 1970s have been described as the era of 'free enterprise' in the charismatic renewal movement. Self-appointed bodies sprang up everywhere. American influence increased with men such as Ern Baxter, Bob Mumford, Charles Simpson and Derek Prince coming over here to minister. In the earlier days of the renewal movement the giving of testimonies was the order of the day but as time went on the call was for teaching. This resulted in the founding of the Holy Spirit Teaching Mission centred in Fort Lauderdale, Florida. Controversial elements soon came to the fore. Derek Prince published a book on believers' baptism; the Fort Lauderdale leaders stressed 'discipline', 'shepherding' and 'covering', and words such as 'submission' and 'authority' were frequently heard.

From the outset the renewal movement has known no denominational frontiers. From about 1967 Roman Catholics became greatly influenced by it, and an international charismatic conference in Rome in 1975 organized by Roman Catholic charismatics was attended by some 10,000 people.

It is hardly surprising that many Christians find themselves in a state of confusion. They are conscious something unusual has been going on in the church but they do not know how to assess it. To add to the confusion, they read contradictory pronouncements coming from the lips of those they have hitherto revered as trusted 'fathers in God'. Thus there are those who write off the charismatic movement as a kind of spiritual aberration, devoid of any lasting significance. Some go so far as to say it is at least in part carnal, fleshly, and even Satanic. Others see it as the answer to the prayers of Christians who have zealously prayed for spiritual revival for years, regarding it as first and foremost a movement of God's Spirit.

Just to add to the confusion, closer investigation reveals considerable differences among those who do claim to have been 'baptized in the Spirit'. Some have chosen to remain in their denominations, others have seceded and formed 'house churches'. But even the house-church movement is not all of a piece. There are those who relate to the so-called 'Bradford' or Harvestime group with their magazine *Restoration* and annual gatherings such as the Dales in Yorkshire and the Downs in Sussex. Others have used the phrase 'Kingdom Life' and relate to Gerald Coates and his team at Cobham in Surrey. Another group is based at Chard in Somerset and yet another is associated with a Pastor North and is sometimes humorously referred to as the 'North Circular'. Other groups remain strictly independent, maintaining their own local autonomy.

Although all these groups emphasize the need for being 'baptized in the Spirit', their other emphases vary considerably. In addition to the various groups mentioned, there are also fellowships within the main-line denominations that uphold 'charismatic' teaching in their particular branch of the church. Just to add to the confusion, it is noticeable that these so-called neo-Pentecostalists have tended to have relatively little contact with the traditional Pentecostal denominations such as the Elim Church, the Assemblies of God and the Apostolic Church, although happily this situation is changing.

On the positive side it should be said that in almost every denomination the influence of the movement has been felt in some measure although probably the greatest impact has been made in the Roman Catholic and Anglican churches and the least among the Christian Brethren and Strict Baptists.

Most would acknowledge that the renewal movement has had a profound influence upon the spiritual life of the church generally. There has been a right and proper emphasis on the priority of worship and with it the call for greater congregational participation. The place of the eldership has once again been brought to the fore in different sections of the church; the importance of spiritual gifts, long since neglected, has been emphasized. Fellowship akin to that experienced in the early church has been rediscovered.

All this is on the credit side, although that is not the whole story. Sadly, when a long neglected truth is rediscovered it often tends to be overplayed, and there are certain aspects of the renewal movement that many feel give cause for concern, and, if pressed too far, could lead to error. These would include the tendency to be exclusive and elitist. This has, in turn, led to some groups virtually becoming new denominations. One can see danger signals here. Like the Brethren movement of the early nineteenth century, the charismatic movement of the twentieth could easily become divided between the 'open' and the 'exclusive'. Authoritarianism poses another potential danger. Just as the exclusive brethren became more and more influenced by the pronouncements of the notorious 'Jim' Taylor, so some charismatics tend to follow slavishly the dictates of those who speak at the various Bible weeks associated with the renewal movement.

Many in the movement believe that through it God is, in these last days, perfecting and uniting his church. This leads, by implication, to the concept of a perfect church, a concept held incidentally by Jehovah's Witnesses, Mormons and the followers of Dr Moon. It is highly questionable whether such a concept has scriptural foundations. The idea of a perfect church on earth is a pipe dream. In the sight of God, as believers, we are accounted righteous but we shall only be in fact pure and holy when Christ comes again—then 'we shall see him as he is and we shall be like him' (1 Jn 3:2). At the same time we do have a responsibility as Christians to endeavour to see that our churches are conducted on New Testament lines and that the membership of them is made up of true rather than nominal believers.

The renewal movement has developed a jargon of its own. They often speak of 'going God's way' and emphasize 'body life'. They look for 'agape relationships' within the fellowship and stress the value of 'house cells'. They see themselves as being primarily engaged in restoring God's ways and patterns to the church in these days. Sometimes the phrase 'new covenant community' is used. In a 'restoration' church stress is laid upon divine government as opposed to 'government by the people for the people'. 'Creativity' is a word often used, covering the various forms in which praise and worship may find expression such as in dance and drama, in mime, through instrumental and choral music, etc. New songs and choruses are constantly being introduced and these are generally favoured in preference to traditional hymns. Basically those in the restoration or renewal movement see themselves as calling God's people back to God's ways. This means among other things submission to spiritual authority, that of God and his delegated leaders. If the church is to be effective, it is rightly argued, its membership must be made up only of viable, participating members. There must be no mere adherents, no peripheral ones. Therefore all potential members must go through a very thorough commitment course before being admitted. In this course, among other things, stress is laid on God's order in the home. Members are placed in house groups or house cells on the understanding they are under the authoritative shepherding of the leader or leaders, or of someone delegated by them. The overall pastor or leading elder is the ultimate head but he will check out every major decision with his fellow elders. The basic assumption is that every man needs another man with delegated authority as a shepherd over his personal life. The church leader is no exception to this—in his case the 'head over the head' may be local or he may be thousands of miles away.

Leaders are selected by existing leaders—they are given graduated responsibility under careful supervision. Not every leader is an elder. Deacons are those with special responsibility for material or practical matters. Men outside the local fellowship but in close touch with it, who have an apostolic function and may even be known as apostles, appoint the elders.

Inevitably the charismatic movement is experience-orientated, but must not be rejected on that account provided experience is always tested by the yardstick of Scripture. We are commanded to worship in spirit and in truth. We must be careful to maintain that our basic authority is found in Scripture and not derived from visions and revelations that may add to or subtract from the teaching of Scripture.

Our main concern, however, is the exclusivism displayed by some charismatics. They tend to have fellowship only with themselves and show at times a sad intolerance for those who do not see things exactly as they do. As there is considerable emphasis on submission to leaders, the tendency is to lop off those who are unwilling to submit. They prefer to have congregations made up of people who have been 'discipled' by them, thus accepting without question everything they have been taught. While this may sound to some unduly strict, it is understandable in the present climate when in all too many churches members are admitted with minimal understanding of the Christian faith.

Changes are discernible within the renewal movement. On the whole there is less emphasis now on speaking in tongues and healing than used to be the case and more on prophecy and teaching. Central meetings tend to be less popular. In earlier years evangelism was rather neglected but this is not so nowadays. Many have participated fully in large-scale missions led by Billy Graham and Luis Palau. A number of charismatic communities have come into being where emphasis is placed on a simpler lifestyle.

One of the most marked features of the renewal movement is its appeal to the younger generation. Those who gather, for example, at the Dales in Yorkshire, or the Downs in Sussex, are for the most part 20- and 30-year-olds. Congregations in churches affected by the movement are largely made up of the same age group. Among young people there seems to be increasing disillusionment with institutional religion whatever form it may take. One is aware at the same time that the freedom enjoyed in charismatic worship, for example, is itself in danger of becoming stereotyped. In the house churches and in many independent charismatic Free Churches the order of service is entirely predictable. A prolonged period of worship which includes a good deal of chorus singing and hand-clapping, the opportunity for speaking in tongues and for prophecy, followed by a message, is the usual pattern. The house-church movement in general is very much male-orientated and the leaders or group leaders are much to the fore. Undoubtedly it is the loving atmosphere and warm fellowship to be experienced in these 'renewed' churches which attracts so many. The more traditional churches have a lot to learn in this respect.

It is our God-given responsibility to 'test the spirits' to see whether they are of God. One is tempted to say of the renewal movement as of the proverbial curate's egg—it is 'good in parts'. There are obvious dangers to which reference has already been made—divisiveness, elitism, authoritarianism, exclusivism. Nevertheless, we must surely acknowledge that there is a great deal that is clearly of God. The church needed to be reminded that it is meant to be a fellowship and not merely an institution, that it consists of all true believers, each of whom has a God-given ministry to perform. We needed to be reminded that the gifts of the Spirit were given to be used and that they did not cease to be at the conclusion of the apostolic age. Congregational participation in worship is a scriptural principle if 1 Corinthians chapter 14 is to have any meaning. The concept of a one-man ministry is rightly being questioned and the need for an eldership needs to be stressed. All such moves are very much on the credit side. We should be ready to acknowledge that the renewal movement represents *part* of what God is doing in the world today and probably the most significant thing. As someone has said, all too many churches have become 'institutionalized museums of respectable tradition instead of mobile ambulances driven by God's ever-moving Spirit'. A younger generation of Christians has understandably found traditional church structures too restrictive for the kind of worship and fellowship for which they are seeking. Leaders in the renewal movement are ready to admit mistakes have been made. The exercise of discipline and authority has sometimes been overplayed, as many will concede. The charge of being schismatic may be true in some cases but in others it is more a question of new wine not being able to exist in the old wineskins. Inevitably leaders of new movements tend to be individualistic and often extreme. Such a charge could have been levelled at John Wesley or William Booth. In spite of its shortcomings, many of us sincerely thank God for the impact of the charismatic movement and earnestly seek to conserve the wheat while brushing aside the chaff. The fact is that within the past two or three decades there has been a fresh outpouring of the Holy Spirit that has crossed denominational barriers and brought a new dimension of spiritual life to many Christians. We recognize there are dangers. As Jonathan Edwards wrote: 'A work of God without stumbling blocks is never to be expected'. Inevitably, such a movement attracts both cranks and charlatans. John Wesley suffered many heartaches because of the foolish antics of some of his followers. Having faced the dangers, though, we must avoid throwing away the baby with the bath water! As far as unity is concerned, the renewal movement has created both a new unity among Christians, but also new divisions. One thing it has clearly proved—that unity will not be achieved by looking for the lowest common denominator or by bureaucratic manipulation, but by the coming together of men and women who have had a touch of God's Spirit upon their lives.

10

Spiritual Unity in Action

In Britain, as in America, there are many so-called para-church organizations. By this we mean societies that are usually interdenominational in character and that operate alongside the churches although largely independent of them. Such societies enable Christians from different branches of the church to pool their resources and work together for the common good. The Bible Society is a prime example of such co-operation. It enjoys the support of a very large cross-section of the Christian church and is the handmaid of all.

Evangelical Christians in particular have helped to proliferate the number of these interdenominational societies. Some, such as Scripture Union and the Universities and Colleges Christian Fellowship, have a wide appeal and cover work of considerable diversity. Many overseas missionary societies are also interdenominational in character although some would prefer to be regarded as non-denominational. A large proportion of work among young people is of a similar character—Boys and Girls Brigade, British Youth for Christ, Covenanters, Campaigners, Christian Endeavour, Crusaders; none of these organizations is linked with any one denomination.

A great many societies operate in this way. Some

would say 'too many'! Although Christians pay lip-service to the slogan 'spiritual unity in action', there is a degree of duplication and even of competition. There are, for example, about half a dozen different societies involved in evangelistic work among the Jews, and a similar number of societies committed to upholding the Protestant faith. Doctrinally it would be difficult to find where they are at variance, although when it comes to methods of working differences may occur.

There must be nearly a hundred societies in Britain representing missionary work overseas. Some of these are denominational in character, but a large number are interdenominational. The larger societies are linked with the Conference of British Missionary Societies which, in turn, has ecumenical links but almost all the evangelical societies are in membership of the Evangelical Missionary Alliance. The EMA not only provides a forum for discussing matters of mutual concern but it encourages practical co-operation among its member societies. It also includes Bible, theological and missionary training colleges in its membership.

Work among children is an area that has demonstrated the value of co-operation. There are several organizations that provide teaching material for use in Sunday schools that bears no denominational bias. Gospel Light, Scripture Press and Scripture Union also arrange training courses for Sunday school teachers on an interdenominational basis.

Societies concerned to meet the needs of deprived and underprivileged children abound and most of these are interdenominational. Among them we might mention the Shaftesbury Society and Dr Barnardo's homes. Christians have come together to meet all kinds of human need. One of the most noteworthy 'success' stories of the post-war era has been the growth of the Evangelical Alliance Relief Fund (TEAR Fund). It was launched in World Refugee Year (1961) largely to meet a demand from Christians that they might have an outlet for their giving that was in sympathy with their own theological standpoint. At first the monies that became available were reckoned in hundreds of pounds but today Tear Fund has an annual turnover of over £5,000,000. Among the earliest recipients of help from the Fund were Archdeacon and Mrs Donnithorne for their work in Hong Kong, and also Gladys Aylward. TEAR Fund is probably one of the best modern examples of the value and effectiveness of spiritual unity in action.

The names of some of the older societies sound a little strange to our modern ears and in some cases these have been changed—Aged Pilgrims' Friends Society, Distressed Gentlefolks Aid Association, the Society for the Assistance of Ladies in Reduced Circumstances—hardly the titles we would choose were those societies coming into being today.

In the nineteenth century there was a plethora of societies promoting temperance in the use of alcohol or total abstinence from it. In 1853 the United Kingdom Alliance was organized to encourage the passage of all forms of legislation aimed to restrict the liquor traffic. The National Temperance League, formed in 1856, commended itself to a number of evangelicals. The United Kingdom Band of Hope Union, formed in 1835, has a definitely Christian foundation. The movement has always concerned itself for the general spiritual well-being of young people, but, at the same time, emphasizing the evils of alcohol. Among the other temperance societies mention should be made of the National British Women's Total Abstinence Union. The work of this society has included the provision of 'dry' canteens for working men in various towns and cities. Most of the large denominations, of course, also have their own temperance groups or societies. In an age when alcoholism is a growing problem, particularly among the young, some of these societies may well enjoy a new lease of life.

In the field of providing training on an interdenominational basis evangelical Christians have probably been most significantly successful. Most of the Bible Colleges are full to capacity and in this respect they compare rather favourably with many of their denominational counterparts. North of the border, the Bible Training Institute has an honourable record of training men and women for service both at home and abroad. The same could be said of 'Lebanon', the missionary Bible College at Berwick on Tweed, and of the Birmingham Bible Institute, Moorlands Bible College in Dorset and the South Wales Bible College. It was just prior to the Second World War that several Christian leaders met in London to discuss the need for having a Bible College in the metropolis. It was resolved that such a college should operate at a high academic level but remain unswervingly loyal to the supreme and final authority of Scripture. As the war drew to a close the London Bible College emerged and today with well over 200 full-time students it is the largest college of its kind in Europe. An exciting development in missionary training took place when three colleges—All Nations, Mount Hermon and Ridgelands—came together to form the All Nations Christian College with its base at Easnye, near Ware in Hertfordshire.

Christians have traditionally concerned themselves with specific groups of people in the community such as those in the services, in industry, in the professions and in prison. Those 'who go down to the sea in ships' seem to have received particular attention with such societies as Agnes Weston's Royal Sailors' Rests, the Seamen's Christian Friend Society, British Sailors' Society and the Royal National Mission to Deep Sea Fishermen. Civil Servants, Post Office employees, railway workers, police, commercial travellers all have societies geared to cater for their particular spiritual needs. One of the most recent societies to capture the imagination and support of the Christian public is the Prison Christian Fellowship which already has a remarkable record of effective work among the prison population.

One could go on indefinitely listing the so-called 'voluntary societies', most of which cross denominational barriers and provide examples of 'spiritual unity in action'. In 1951—Festival of Britain year—a United Exhibition was held in London, sponsored by the Evangelical Alliance, at which no less than 180 societies demonstrated their work. Admittedly one gained the impression that there was a certain amount of duplication but overall it was a powerful testimony of what may be achieved when Christians get together and pool their resources.

It is not, of course, only or even primarily at the

national level that 'spiritual unity in action' is best demonstrated. In many areas groups of local churches have come together to provide facilities that no one local church would be able to provide—homes for old people, youth centres, telephone counselling ministry and various specialized training courses. A healthy 'togetherness' should always find some practical expression since 'togetherness' is never an end in itself. Christians are coming to see more and more that duplication of effort is not only wasteful but often positively unChristian. The Festival of Light, now renamed Care Trust, which reached its peak in the early 1970s, represents the strength of the silent majority when they unitedly drew attention to moral and social issues.

While many of us pay lip-service to the concept of spiritual unity in action, we have to face the fact that even Christians can be guilty of 'empire building'. All too often people who are one in doctrine find it hard to co-operate in some piece of Christian work. Many have a sneaking feeling the job will be done better if they 'go it alone'. Sadly, it is sometimes a case of strong personalities wanting their own way and being unwilling to team up with others holding similar theological views but perhaps differing on minor points of procedure. Nevertheless, a great deal of good is being done through the aegis of the voluntary societies which even in a 'day of small things' continue to proliferate.

In recent years there has been a marked increase in the number of interdenominational conventions. Each year Christians gather in their thousands for such events as the Keswick Convention, Filey Christian Holiday Week, now at Skegness, Royal Week and

Spring Harvest. Although predominantly supported by the house churches, many from the more traditional churches support the annual Bible weeks at the Dales in Yorkshire, the Downs in Sussex, the New Forest and other centres. It is not difficult to produce evidence of spiritual unity in action both at the essentially spiritual level as well as in various practical and humanitarian ways.

11

Expressions of Unity

In Britain there are several organizations that seek to promote co-operation between Christians of different denominations. Some reference to this has already been made in Chapter 5, but here we shall examine the subject in more detail.

The British Council of Churches is the national expression of the ecumenical movement and is linked directly with the World Council, sharing the same doctrinal basis—'a fellowship of churches in the British Isles which confess the Lord Jesus Christ as God and Saviour according to the Scriptures and therefore seek to fulfil together their common calling to the glory of the one God, Father, Son and Holy Spirit'.

The BCC was formed in 1942 through the amalgamation of several existing ecumenical-type bodies. It links together the mainline non-Roman denominations. The Roman Catholic Church sends observers to the meetings. In different parts of the country there are local Councils of Churches in association with the BCC. The 'Week of Prayer for Christian Unity' held every January is sponsored by the BCC. The various member churches elect members to the Council, which normally meets in full session twice a year. Christian Aid is a department of the Council.

At the other end of the spectrum is the British Evangelical Council which describes itself as a council of ecumenically uncompromised evangelical churches, one in the gospel. It was formed in 1952 with the Fellowship of Independent Evangelical Churches (founded in 1922) as one of its founder members. It has a clearly defined doctrinal basis:

> The inerrancy of the Holy Scriptures as originally given, their verbal inspiration by God and their supreme authority as the only rule of faith and practice.
>
> The trinity of the Godhead; Father, Son and Holy Spirit, Who are the same in substance, equal in power and glory.
>
> The essential, absolute and eternal Deity of the Lord Jesus Christ; His conception by the Holy Ghost; His birth of the virgin Mary, His real but sinless humanity; His voluntary humiliation in life as a Man of Sorrows culminating in His substitutionary and atoning death as a sacrifice for sin; His resurrection from the dead on the third day in that very body that had lain in the tomb; His ascension into heaven as the only Mediator between God and man and His coming again in power and glory.
>
> The personality and deity of the Holy Spirit through whom the soul is born again to saving repentance and faith and by whom the saints are sanctified through the truth.
>
> Man's utter ruin through the fall and his salvation solely by grace through faith in Jesus Christ, whose righteousness imputed to him is the only ground of acceptance before God.
>
> The resurrection of the body, the judgement of the world by our Lord Jesus Christ, the everlasting blessedness of the saved and the everlasting punishment of the lost.

> The spiritual unity of all who truly believe in the Lord Jesus Christ and their duty to maintain in themselves and in the Church a standard of life and doctrine that is in conformity with the teaching of God's Holy Word.

The British Evangelical Council in an official policy statement also makes its position quite clear:

> The British Evangelical Council was formed to draw together those churches which are one on the fundamental doctrines of the faith, which desire to discover and experience that true ecumenicity which the Scriptures certainly teach, and which are therefore also united in their opposition to the development of that form of unscriptural ecumenicity represented by the World Council of Churches.
>
> We believe that for evangelical churches outwardly to remain in fellowship with the World Council of Churches or any of its associated bodies by, for instance, remaining within the doctrinally-mixed denominations affiliated to it is contrary to scriptural principles. Thereby the Gospel is compromised, if not denied, since such is an attempt to achieve organizational union at the expense of vital Christian truths, and the expression of a true evangelical unity in a fellowship at church level is grievously hindered.
>
> By its ambiguity and permitted latitude of interpretation the doctrinal basis of the World Council of Churches, so far from being an adequate safeguard against heresy, is rather a cover for it so that within its ranks are found church bodies who hold modernist, sacramentarian and even unitarian views. For ourselves we cannot be associated in any way with a movement which implies that the evangelical position is but one of many insights or traditions and which necessarily requires evangelical churches, directly or indirectly associated with it, to be

> in fellowship as fellow-Christian churches with religious bodies which do not hold to the very essentials of biblical Christianity.

Among the denominational and other groups affiliated to the Council are the Free Church of Scotland, the Evangelical Movement of Wales, the Metropolitan Association of Strict Baptist Churches and the Evangelical Fellowship of Congregational churches.

The British Evangelical Council holds an Annual Conference as well as occasional study conferences and publishes a theological journal called *Foundations*. Although not its official organ, the views of British Evangelical Council members find expression in the monthly paper *Evangelical Times*.

In between the all-inclusive British Council of Churches and the very exclusive British Evangelical Council is the Evangelical Alliance, founded in 1846, linking together evangelical Christians—whether in the so-called mainline denominations or in the independent groups. It has a similar basis of faith to the British Evangelical Council which is presented in this way:

> Evangelical Christians accept the revelation of the triune God given in the Scriptures of the Old and New Testaments and confess the historic faith of the gospel therein set forth. They here assert doctrines which they regard as crucial to the understanding of the faith, and which should issue in mutual love, practical Christian service and evangelistic concern:
>
> The sovereignty and grace of God the Father, God the Son and God the Holy Spirit in creation, providence, revelation, redemption and final judgement.

The divine inspiration of Holy Scripture and its consequent entire trustworthiness and supreme authority in all matters of faith and conduct.

The universal sinfulness and guilt of fallen man, making him subject to God's wrath and condemnation.

The substitutionary sacrifice of the incarnate Son of God as the sole and all-sufficient ground of redemption from the guilt and power of sin, and from its eternal consequences.

The justification of the sinner solely by the grace of God through faith in Christ crucified and risen from the dead.

The illuminating, regenerating, indwelling and sanctifying work of God the Holy Spirit.

The priesthood of all believers, who form the universal church, the Body of which Christ is the Head, and which is committed by His command to the proclamation of the Gospel throughout the world.

The expectation of the personal, visible return of the Lord Jesus Christ in power and glory.

Evangelism has always been a primary concern of the Alliance which has its own Department of Evangelism. The Evangelical Alliance was responsible for inviting Dr Billy Graham to conduct his first major crusade in Britain in 1954. Its other activities have included the launching of Tear Fund; running a hostel for overseas students in North London; the setting up of the Arts Centre Group and the sponsorship and subsequent publication of major reports on various topics related to mission and evangelism.

Through its many contacts the Evangelical Alliance acts as a watchman for evangelical interests and a spokesman for the evangelical cause. Information of all kinds is provided: from the beliefs of newly arrived cults to the whereabouts of a local evangelical church.

The Alliance was responsible for bringing into being the Evangelical Missionary Alliance and brings together almost all of Britain's full-time evangelists at an annual conference in December.

As well as having individuals in membership, the Evangelical Alliance links together local churches, area fellowships and societies and through its Council and various sub-committees promotes co-operation among those who share a common evangelical faith.

The fact that there are two organizations in being with almost identical doctrinal bases and both purporting to be acting in the interests of evangelical unity highlights the tragedy of our divisiveness. Brethren who are truly one in Christ find themselves divided at church level on account of different attitudes to the ecumenical movement. The one ray of hope is to be found in the fact that leaders in these different groups are now getting together informally once a year to discuss the points at issue.

There are of course numerous other bodies working for unity among Christians at differing levels. One such is the Order for Christian Unity which is more broadly based than the Evangelical Alliance. It was founded in 1950 by Mr Ernest Tapp, a Methodist layman, because he believed that Christians from all denominations increasingly wished to work together to uphold Christian values for the common good while at the same time remaining entirely faithful to their own denominations. In order to safeguard against division over doctrinal issues, the Order lays it down that members should adhere absolutely to the forms of worship, doctrinal interpretations and authority of their own denomination.

The Order of Christian Unity is mainly concerned to uphold Christian ethical standards and to counter the challenge being made by secular and anti-Christian forces. Thus the Order addresses itself to such tasks as promoting and defending Christian education in state schools, providing responsible sex education for schoolchildren, upholding Christian standards of marriage, raising the standards of television and radio programmes and opposing abortion on demand and euthanasia.

There are of course other interdenominational groups with similar objectives—such as Care Trust and the Shaftesbury Project. The issue is often raised as to how far Christians need to be at one over doctrinal matters when facing the challenge of anti-Christian ethical teaching and practice. One thing is certain: when Christians stand shoulder to shoulder in any particular enterprise, be it evangelism or upholding standards of morality, they do sense increasingly their oneness in Christ.

12

Accent on Youth

In the years following World War II the accent was placed fairly and squarely on youth. The British Government voted considerable sums of money in order to get work among young people started at local level. Youth committees were set up and full-time youth officers appointed. Gymnastic and other facilities were provided. Voluntary organizations, including those attached to churches, benefited in that they were able to obtain equipment either freely or at minimum cost. For some years local youth clubs flourished, catering for teenage groups. As time went on, however, the appeal of these clubs waned and the average age level fell considerably. The basic reason was probably lack of incentive. What was the real point of it all? The war was over and there seemed little to capture the imagination of young people. We had the 'spivs', the 'Teddy boys' with their Edwardian dress, the 'mods' and 'rockers', the 'greasers', 'skinheads', 'Hell's angels', 'punks'—different names but all applicable to successive generations of young people who had lost their way and yet were trying to find a means of expressing themselves.

The churches turned their attention to young people with varying degrees of success. Since long before the war there had been various national organizations, uniformed and non-uniformed, denominational and interdenominational, but their appeal was and still is limited. Many churches started youth clubs on similar lines to secular clubs, except that in most cases they sought to include a short epilogue in the programme. It is questionable how much has, in fact, been achieved by this means, but some would say at least they have kept youngsters 'off the streets'. The churches, like the State, found their appeal was to the lower age groups. Few in their late teens or early twenties were interested.

In the immediate post-war years Youth for Christ became well established in Britain, concentrating particularly on monthly evangelistic rallies. The various youth movements, Crusaders and Covenanters, Pathfinders and King's Own, attracted considerable support. Uniformed movements such as the Boys' and Girls' Brigades and Campaigners also carried on with a fair measure of success.

In the late 1960s a movement arose which appealed to the very people on whom the churches had so far made little impact—the 'Jesus Movement'. There was a time when it was confidently predicted that this would sweep through Britain as it had in many areas of the United States. While this did not in fact occur, the influence of the movement has undoubtedly been felt over here. The Jesus Movement was born at a time when a large segment of American youth was experimenting with mind-bending drugs, protesting against the Vietnam war, and seeking devious escape routes from the prevailing materialism of the West. There were the 'flower people' proclaiming love and peace, but with little doctrinal substance to their message.

The churches were tragically ineffective in communicating the gospel to these young people. They were too respectable, too hidebound by tradition. Many young people were disillusioned by the fact that, although their parents professed to believe in God, they were in reality worshipping at the shrine of materialism. Religion was associated with getting dressed in a suit, wearing a collar and tie and shaking hands with old people. In his book *The Jesus Movement* Dr Billy Graham enumerated some of the main characteristics of 'the Jesus people'. He pointed out that the movement was essentially Bible-based and Christ-centred. There was also a renewed emphasis on the Holy Spirit, although by no means all of the Jesus people could be described as 'neo-Pentecostalists'. They were genuinely concerned about the implications of Christian discipleship and had a real sense of social responsibility. Perhaps the most significant feature of all in the movement was the incredible zeal for evangelism which was so evident, together with a sense that the time was short and that Christ's return was imminent.

It is dangerous to make generalizations about a movement made up of so many different strands. The Jesus people had their extremists and there was in some quarters the danger of personality cults developing. It was usually this aspect which was mentioned in the secular press.

As far as Britain was concerned the first 'Jesus Tents' appeared at various pop festivals in 1969, but it was in 1971 that we came face to face with the real Jesus people. This was the year of the Festival of Light with its campaign for 'positive virtues' and its crusade against moral pollution. Among those who visited

Britain at this time were Americans Arthur Blessitt and Lornie Frisbee. Blessitt, the 'Minister of Sunset Strip', appeared with very long hair and extremely trendy clothes, and his messages were very much to the point. Lornie Frisbee, an artist turned 'Jesus freak', declared: 'These are the last days, and God is sweeping over the country.' Undoubtedly something of the Jesus Movement brushed off onto the younger members of the Christian public in Britain. It is unfortunate that some have judged the whole movement by the activities of the 'Children of God', an extremist group which gained an undue amount of press and television publicity. Few communes were set up in Britain. One could almost say that the Jesus Movement became anglicized.

We have had our spate of Christian 'pop groups' too. At one time we faced a rash of Christian 'stickers' bidding us 'Smile, Jesus loves you'. *Buzz* magazine has consistently given good coverage of the activities of this younger generation of Christians. Some young people adopted for a while the 'One Way' Jesus salute. The Jesus Liberation Front emerged and lasted for a few years as a kind of 'service' organization for young people supplying very much 'with it' material for evangelism—badges, stickers, posters, tracts. Innate British conservatism, to say nothing of a sense of reverence for holy things, however, reacted against the phraseology used in certain quarters. The average British Christian, even the modern teenager, hesitates to describe himself as 'stoned on Jesus', or on 'a Jesus trip'.

Nevertheless, one can truly thank God for much that has happened on the youth scene. Spree '73 held at Earls Court, London, bore witness to the influence of the Jesus Movement on young people in Britain. No one could doubt their sincerity, and their evangelistic zeal would put many an older Christian to shame, yet at the same time they bore the stamp of their generation. They had discovered the heart of the Christian message and yet escaped some of the impediments of its conventional trappings.

The reaction of the official churches as well as of some ultra-conservative evangelicals remains 'sceptical', yet most would have to admit in all honesty that these young people have had much to teach the 'established' churches. They represent a genuine attempt to rediscover basic New Testament Christian faith which all too often has been obscured by ecclesiastical accretions and traditions.

In Britain one group of 'Jesus people' formed themselves into a loose fellowship under the name of Outreach for Jesus. One of the leading figures among them was Jim Palosaari, a young American, who later returned to the United States. They were responsible for putting on music concerts with 'the Sheep', a Christian rock group. They also took to different parts of the country a multi-media dramatic presentation called 'Lonesome Stone'. A Christian businessman, a former member of the 'Exclusive' Brethren, Mr Kenneth P. Frampton, took a particular interest in their activities.

For several years now there has been held in the summer a Christian arts festival known as Greenbelt. It is probably one of the largest gatherings of young Christians held in the course of the year. It is described as 'a celebration of God-given creativity'. Music, drama, dance, films and poetry all have their place. One wonders if such a gathering would ever have taken place apart from the long-term influence of the Jesus Movement.

The Jesus Movement in Britain has not been as easily definable nor as obvious as its counterpart in America. Nevertheless there are today thousands of young people who are not ashamed to confess Christ openly but who revolt against the idea that Christianity should be equated with conventional dress and middle class 'respectability'.

Such epithets as 'superficial', 'irreverent' and 'cheap' have been levelled at some of the young people who have been caught up in this Movement. Evangelists working with gospel 'beat' or 'rock' groups have frequently been accused of failing to declare 'the whole counsel of God' and doubts have been cast on the genuineness of those who have made professions of faith. Some of these accusations are certainly justifiable, yet they have a hollow ring about them when uttered by those who themselves have little or no active personal involvement in the work of evangelism.

Two musicals staged in London theatres—*Godspell* and *Jesus Christ Superstar*—met with astounding popularity. *Godspell* in particular enjoyed a good press, and many leading clerics, including Dr Ramsey, a former Archbishop of Canterbury, commended it. On the other hand, the fact that Jesus is portrayed in the guise of a clown understandably evoked the criticism of many Christians. The script of the play was nevertheless almost wholly taken from the Bible.

Most would agree that *Jesus Christ Superstar* fell into a different category from *Godspell*. Here our Lord is represented as someone who is the victim of his own publicity—'a ranting neurotic, borne along by the adulation of his followers'—to quote Michael Jacob's comment in *Pop Goes Jesus*. Even more remarkable than the box office appeal of these musicals was the fact that one of John Newton's hymns should have been a few years ago 'top of the pops'. The words of 'Amazing Grace' may be far removed from contemporary language, but it was a hit!

What are we to say to these things? Are we to read into the situation that Britain is on the way to a great spiritual reawakening? No one can answer that. That there is a growing interest in the supernatural is beyond question. Unfortunately this all too often takes on a sinister form, with the result that in recent years there has been renewed attention given by young people to witchcraft, the occult and Satanism. Oxford Street, as well as other town centres, has been invaded by the adherents of Hare Krishna. Christians nevertheless do well to capitalize on this new openness to the supernatural. Those who feel that the gospel must be presented in such a way that it will truly be communicated to this generation should not be condemned out of hand because they depart from seventeenth-century English and Victorian methodology. If the truth that Jesus is alive today is to be conveyed meaningfully, then we must speak in language that the common people will understand. For too long there has been an unnecessary generation gap in the field of evangelism. There are those who feel that evangelism must be conducted solely on traditional lines, virtually in the context of what is tantamount to a church service, while others call for an entirely new approach, using music that is more likely to make a popular appeal. Of course gospel groups as we have known them for several years will in due time be as dated as the 'skiffle groups' which appeared at evangelistic meetings in the years immediately after World War II.

> Our little systems have their day,
> They have their day and cease to be.

Whatever changes may take place in the methods of presenting the gospel, the truth of its message remains constant and each succeeding generation must measure up to its responsibility—'by all means to save some'.

There are in Britain a growing number of societies and organizations which are primarily concerned to reach young people with the gospel. In recent years British Youth for Christ has enjoyed a new lease of life, first under the direction of Clive Calver and later Rob White. 'Spring Harvest' at Pontin's Camp, Prestatyn was launched in April 1979 as a joint enterprise between BYFC and *Buzz* magazine and provided a training programme for 3,000 young people. By 1984 it covered three consecutive weeks and catered for 20,000 people. It is a fact that in most churches which could truthfully be described as 'alive' today, young people preponderate. The greatest response at evangelistic campaigns is among young people. When it comes to Christian unity young people have a lot to teach older Christians. Few of them have any denominational hang-ups and find no problem in linking up with others from different denominational backgrounds.

13

The Wider World

During the last four decades there have been several Congresses on Evangelism at the international level in which Christian leaders from Britain have participated. The first such Congress was held in Berlin in November 1966 and was sponsored by *Christianity Today*, the American theological journal of which Dr Carl Henry was then Editor-in-Chief. Dr Billy Graham was Honorary Chairman of the Congress which drew over 1,200 delegates to Berlin from scores of countries across the world. Many saw this Congress as being a counterpart in modern times to the World Missionary Conference held in Edinburgh in 1910.

The slogan of the Berlin Congress was 'One Race, One Gospel, One Task'. On 'Reformation Sunday' which fell during the Congress, the delegates, joined by more than 10,000 Berliners, marched through the centre of the city to join in a service of Christian witness, which was addressed by Billy Graham. Two other interesting features of the Congress were the presence of Emperor Haile Selassie I of Ethiopia and of two converted Auca Indians from Amazonia. Among the many speakers, Britain was represented by the Rev John Stott, whose theme was 'The Great Commission'.

One feature of the Congress was a series of addresses entitled 'Windows on the World', in which nationals from nearly forty different areas spoke of the religious situation in their part of the world.

Britishers played a full and active part in the Congress at all levels and undoubtedly the Congress proved to be to many a stimulus to renewed evangelistic activity. Words spoken by Dr Carl Henry at the Congress find an echo in our hearts over a decade later: 'Outside a rediscovery of the gospel of grace there now remains no long-range prospect for the survival of modern civilization, but only a guarantee of its utter collapse.'

Mention should be made of EURO' 70—Billy Graham's television crusade based in Dortmund in West Germany—'eight days when the miracle of modern technology projected the Christian message across Europe'. This was the comment of Dave Foster who was deeply involved in the project and who has since written up the whole story. By means of the largest closed-circuit TV network ever attempted in Europe, the American evangelist addressed an aggregate total of some 800,000 people in ten different countries. Although only two towns in Britain (Chatham and Port Talbot) made arrangements to take the telecast, Britishers had a very important part to play in the whole operation. Businessman and electronics engineer David Rennie was the genius overseeing the technical side of the operation, while Dave Foster undertook a mammoth task in the area of publicity.

EURO' 70 was fresh in the minds of those responsible for planning the European Congress on Evangelism in 1971. Earlier, in 1969, Billy Graham had invited a group of Christian leaders to meet him in Paris in order to discuss the possibility of such a Congress. I was asked to head up an Executive Committee with Peter Schneider of Berlin as Vice-Chairman. No less than ten different European countries were represented on the Committee. Invaluable help in administration was generously provided by the Billy Graham Evangelistic Association. One of the important features of the Congress was the proliferation of 'mini-conferences', each related to some particular aspect of evangelistic activity. The organizers made a strenuous effort to get younger people to Amsterdam, and they were largely successful. One evening was given over to a youth presentation in which Cliff Richard featured.

Although the European Congress was largely underwritten financially by American Christians, there were definitely no strings attached. The organizing committee was left entirely free to make all the arrangements. Billy Graham himself had to be pressed to take any prominent part in the programme.

The Amsterdam Congress proved a stimulus to evangelistic activity in many areas, especially in countries where evangelical Christians are very much in a minority and suffering certain disabilities as far as their witness is concerned.

In July 1974 a second International Congress on World Evangelization was held in Lausanne, Switzerland. The Congress was arranged in response to a request from over a hundred Christian leaders from all over the world and planning for it was in the hands of a thoroughly representative International Committee under the chairmanship of Bishop A. Jack Dain of

Sydney, Australia. It was agreed from the outset that this Congress should have a limited number of plenary sessions, leaving ample time for smaller working groups to meet.

Those responsible for planning the Lausanne Congress had sought to ensure that it should be more representative of evangelical Christianity worldwide than any other gathering in modern times. Every person invited was selected by the planning committee on his or her individual merits. An endeavour was made to see that half of those present were under 45 years of age with the aim that up to 20% should be under 30. Regardless of age, sex, geographical location or type of work, every participant was required to be a committed Christian in full sympathy with the evangelical position and with the potential to influence a sizable section of the Christian community in his own country after the Congress. Billy Graham was honorary chairman and among the main speakers were the Rev. G. Osei-Mensah of Kenya; Dr Susanna Uda of Japan, Dr Rene Padilla of Argentina, and the Rev. John Stott from London; Professor Peter Beyerhaus of Germany, Bishop Festo Kivengere of Uganda, Dr Donald McGavran of USA, Canon Michael Green, at the time Principal of St John's College, Nottingham; Professor Henri Blocher of France, Samuel Escobar, a Latin American on the Inter-Varsity staff and Dr Francis Schaeffer of L'Abri, Switzerland; Dr George Peters of USA, and Dr Howard Snyder of Brazil. A number of Britons were involved in the various training and workshop sessions, including Ernest Oliver, then General Secretary of the Evangelical Missionary Alliance. I list these names just to illustrate the international flavour of the Congress, showing as it does that Christians can unite across the continents when the need is justified.

And how justified it was! The main thrust of the Congress was the church's urgent need to complete the unfinished task of world evangelization before the end of the present century. From the start, it had been viewed as a part of a process rather than as an event in itself. What happened before and after the Congress was considered to be as important as what happened during the ten days of the Congress itself.

British Christians tend to be somewhat sceptical regarding the value of congresses of this kind, which involve so much organization and expense. Lausanne had its critics not all of whom had been well-informed. It is not difficult to point to significant returns from Berlin 1966 and Amsterdam 1971. Some may feel that there are too many conferences these days, but at least the coming together of Christian leaders to discuss matters of vital importance has precedent in Scripture! (E.g. Acts chapter 15.) Perhaps in the past we in Britain have been a little too self-sufficient. The moral and spiritual state of Britain would surely indicate that we should be ready to learn all we can from as many different quarters as possible, in order that, by God's help, we may more adequately be the means of pointing men and women to the only answer to their need—the Lord Jesus Christ.

The 'findings' of the Lausanne Congress were largely incorporated in a Covenant which was presented to the participants by John Stott on the last evening of the Congress. They were invited, if they so wished, to sign the Covenant as an expression of their sympathy with its declarations.

There was in the Covenant an unequivocal statement about the uniqueness of Christ—his person and his work. The nature of true evangelism was clearly set forth: 'Evangelism is the proclamation of the historical, biblical Christ as Saviour and Lord, with a view to persuading people to come to him personally and so be reconciled to God.'

The relationship between the gospel and its social implications was also spelt out. Lausanne marked a step forward on the part of evangelicals as far as social awareness is concerned—'When people receive Christ they are born again into his kingdom and must seek not only to exhibit but also to spread its righteousness in the midst of an unrighteous world. The salvation we claim should be transforming us in the totality of our personal and social responsibilities. Faith without works is dead.'

'Triumphalism' was for the most part conspicuous by its absence at Lausanne. There was a good deal of heart-searching and not a little penitence. Evangelicals were challenged to develop a simpler life-style in order that their witness might be more effective.

In countries such as Britain with a Christian heritage of many centuries, the need for the church to be revitalized and to be freed from the dead hand of mere traditionalism was stressed again and again.

One could not help feeling that much had happened since Berlin in 1966. Time alone will show how much of the forward-thinking expressed at Lausanne will yet percolate through to the rank-and-file church member. It is to be regretted that a larger number of evangelical leaders from Britain were not present at the Congress since there was much there which was relevant to the British scene.

The initiative represented by the Lausanne Congress has since been carried forward by the Lausanne Committee for World Evangelization—a cross-section of leaders representative of evangelical thinking across the world. A consultation on World Evangelization was held in January 1980 in Thailand, bringing together some 500 participants, selected on a regional basis. This gathering gave further impetus to biblical evangelism worldwide as well as an opportunity to share insights gained and progress made since Lausanne 1974. Then in 1983 under the overall chairmanship of Billy Graham a world congress of itinerant evangelists was held in Amsterdam.

These are some of the examples of togetherness at world level which have taken place in our time. Modern means of communication have made getting together almost anywhere in the world a relatively simple exercise.

It is significant that, whether at the local, national or international level, Christians seem to find one subject in particular that is most likely to bring them together: evangelism. It is as we look out that we find a genuine spirit of unity within the body of Christ.

14

Together in Glory

Many years ago I came across a rather quaint poem entitled 'No Sect in Heaven'. This may sound a little strange to our modern ears but its essential message is true—there will be 'no sect in heaven'.

To think of segregation in heaven is impossible since there the family of God will be complete, 'a radiant church, without stain or wrinkle or any other blemish' (Eph 5:27). There we shall all lose our labels and be 'all one in Christ Jesus'. Many of us look back with fond memories to those occasions here on earth when we have gathered for worship with Christians from different denominations and from varying cultural backgrounds—it has been a little foretaste of heaven as we have been 'lost in wonder, love and praise'.

Togetherness finds its ultimate fulfilment in heaven. Jesus pictured the day when 'many will come from the east and the west, and will take their places at the feast with Abraham, Isaac and Jacob in the kingdom of heaven' (Mt 8:11). In the book of Revelation we are given a further glimpse of the oneness that will characterize the saints in glory—the redeemed will be there from 'every tribe and language and people and nation' (Rev 5:9) and, dare we add, denomination? There is certainly no suggestion of sectarianism in heaven.

There the unity we wistfully pursue on earth will be fully realized. The measure of togetherness we feel when we meet here on earth marks the degree to which we gain a foretaste of heaven in the here and now.

Isaiah, in one of his messianic prophecies regarding the kingdom age, pictures a day when seemingly incompatible creatures will dwell together happily:

> The wolf will live with the lamb, the leopard will lie down with the goat, the calf and the lion and the yearling together; and a little child will lead them. The cow will feed with the bear, their young will lie down together, and the lion will eat straw like the ox. The infant will play near the hole of the cobra, and the young child put his hand into the viper's nest. They will neither harm nor destroy on all my holy mountain, for the earth will be full of the knowledge of the Lord as the waters cover the sea (Is 11:6–9).

When God reigns supreme, whether in heaven or on earth, strife and discord disappear.

Heaven has been described as 'a prepared place for a prepared people'. It is certainly a realm where every disagreeable element is missing—'nothing impure will ever enter it, nor will anyone who does what is shameful or deceitful, but only those whose names are written in the Lamb's book of life' (Rev 21:27). The Apostle Paul lists some of the categories of people who would not be acceptable—'neither the sexually immoral nor idolaters nor adulterers nor male prostitutes nor homosexual offenders nor thieves nor the greedy nor drunkards nor slanderers nor swindlers' (1 Cor 6:10). At the same time he reminds the church at Corinth that before they were converted many of them were just such people. We are all 'sinners saved by grace' but our salvation will not be complete until we see Christ face to face and then and only then will we be truly like him. At that point we are fit for heaven because all trace of sin will have been removed from us. At the root of all discord and disharmony lies the ugly fact of sin. We see this at the very beginning—the sin of Adam and Eve brought estrangement from God and before long their two sons were at variance with one another. Sin is the root cause of the world's unrest. Sin keeps people apart. Even in Christians it is sin that brings discord—pride, self-assertiveness, intolerance, jealousy, prejudice.

When we enjoy a real sense of togetherness here on earth there is always at the back of our minds the question as to how long it will last. We attend a conference or a convention and we feel spiritually refreshed—the sense of oneness thrills us, but the week passes all too quickly and we return to the usual routine. Or it may be in the local church we reach a depth of fellowship that approximates to that described by Luke in the early chapters of Acts. While it lasts we enjoy it, it is heavenly but we have a sneaking feeling it is 'too good to be true', it cannot last. In contrast, the sense of togetherness that we shall know in heaven will endure, nothing will ever detract from it.

The Victorians indulged in sentimental pictures of heavenly bliss but we would do better to restrict ourselves to the limited information the Scriptures provide. For the Christian, heaven is the Father's house (Jn 14:2). Various word pictures combine to present a picture of peace and tranquillity. We look forward to being part of a city whose architect and builder is God (Heb 11:10). A city suggests security and orderliness; that city is also the paradise of God (Rev 2:7). Here the picture is of a beautiful garden, a place of unruffled peace and exquisite beauty. We are left in no doubt about some of the missing elements—'no more night' (Rev 22:5), no hunger, no thirst, no scorching heat (Rev 7:16–17). In other words, the things that bedevil human happiness and peace here on earth are banished from heaven but, above all, heaven will be free from the rivalries and tensions between the people of God that sadly are all too often characteristic of the church on earth.

In every generation groups of earnest Christians have cherished the ideal of a perfect church. They have drawn up rigid doctrinal statements, set high standards of morality and in various ways have sought to ensure that the church shall be wholly free from error. The one thing that has been overlooked is the human propensity to cause division. The result has been that supposedly 'perfect' churches have been split down the middle, often because of personality clashes. Lasting unity appears very elusive. It seems as if it is an unattainable idea, yet that does not absolve us from seeking to maintain unity both in the local fellowship as well as in the churches generally. We are assured of ultimate success since in heaven all divisiveness and rivalry and place-seeking will be no more. There the communion of saints will be fully realized. Communion is conscious oneness:

One army of the living God,
To his command we bow;

Part of his host have crossed the flood,
And part are crossing now.

The great climax of the ages is to be the gathering of the church when Christ returns a second time: 'he will send his angels with a loud trumpet call, and they will gather his elect from the four winds, from one end of the heavens to the other' (Mt 24:31). Those who were believers but who have died will be joined with those alive on earth and together they will meet the Lord in the air (1 Thess 4:16–17). This great gathering will encompass all the redeemed of all the ages. Not one will be overlooked or forgotten. Bigotry and narrow-mindedness will be no more. Party labels will disappear. 'Togetherness' will be witnessed as never before as that 'great multitude which no-one could count, from every nation, tribe, people and language, standing before the throne and in front of the Lamb' (Rev 7:9). The unity that so often eludes us now will be a complete reality in heaven and nothing will ever threaten it.

Oh, then what raptured greetings
On Canaan's happy shore!
What knitting severed friendships up,
Where partings are no more!
Then eyes with joy shall sparkle
That brimmed with tears of late;
Orphans no longer fatherless,
Nor widows desolate.

15

The Pursuit of Unity

The Bible leaves us in no doubt as to the importance of unity. It is something that God desires to see among his people. It was uppermost in the mind of our Lord in his prayer in the Upper Room. While we cannot create unity, we do have a solemn responsibility to maintain it. Furthermore, the unity we are to seek is such that it can be seen by the unbelieving world. Obviously, therefore, there will be a supernatural element about it. In other words it will be different from the kind of unity one might expect to find in an Old Boys' Association, a Women's Institute or a Working Men's Club. Such groupings bring together for the most part people who have a lot in common and who therefore *naturally* gravitate towards one another. Also, the unity expressed in such associations may appear to be very real but is likely on closer examination to be of a somewhat superficial nature. It is not comparable with the oneness that characterized believers in the early church.

While we may pay lip-service to the paramount importance of unity, many of us are not so ready to express it in practice. We may enjoy a considerable oneness within the confines of our own local church and yet have little or nothing to do with fellow

Christians in the locality. At the most we may meet with them two or three times a year—perhaps at a united service in January, a procession of witness on Good Friday and maybe one other occasion in the year. It is true the local ministers may meet more often in 'fraternals' but the church is bigger than its leaders and the times when congregations meet are all too few.

We are not suggesting that local churches should lose their identities but there are many activities that could be carried out corporately rather than in isolation from one another. Could there not be Bible Study groups in the locality from which members of several different churches might profit? From time to time there might be training courses for specific groups within the churches—youth workers, Sunday school teachers, church leaders. Such courses could surely meet the needs of a number of churches rather than just one. There might well be at least a couple of occasions during the year when local congregations meet socially for fellowship, including perhaps a meal together. The young people in churches often show a healthy interest in various forms of sport—football, table tennis, cricket—this could lead to the formation of a local league enabling the different churches to compete with one another on the sports field—instead of spiritually! There are endless possibilities for fostering greater unity at the local level. It usually needs one enterprising person to act as a catalyst. Once a lead is given others are usually ready to follow.

Yet, to be realistic, we know there are those in the churches that shy away from this subject. Their idea of togetherness is strictly confined to their own congregation. To all intents and purposes they are, at least in their own estimation, the only true Christians in the locality. In fact there are those who are immediately suspicious when the subject of unity is raised since they fear it may well be sought at the expense of truth. Then there are those large, prosperous local churches that prefer to go it alone because their own programmes are so full already. They really don't need anyone else. They are self-sufficient. There are local churches that feel that since they and they alone have a full grasp of the truth, to enter into dialogue with others is of questionable value. There are also the strongly denominational churches whose only concept of unity is getting together with other churches of the same faith and order. At the same time there are woolly minded Christians who are prepared for unity at any price. As we have said before, there is a unity we cannot have—with those who preach another gospel.

Two thousand years of church history have conclusively demonstrated that there will always be points of difference among us. We shall not all settle for precisely the same form of church government nor shall we all agree about the nature of the sacraments. The gospel itself is the one great secret of fellowship; outside of it there is no hope of unity. It is totally wrong either to water down our message or compromise our faith for the sake of unity. As Frank Colquhoun wrote many years ago, 'It is only in Christ that we are one; and the Christ in whom we realize our oneness is the Christ of divine revelation: the everlasting Son of the Father, the Lamb of God that takes away the sin of the world, the risen Lord who has led captivity captive and reigns in power at the right hand of the majesty on high'.

If we are to enjoy togetherness we shall need to

distinguish between the essential and the non-essential, between gospel fact and human opinion. We must uphold the right of private judgement, and on some issues it will be a matter of agreeing to differ. There are limits to co-operation but even so we should pursue unity for that is the will of God for his people. Schism is a serious sin; party spirit is an expression of our fallen nature.

In Old Testament times there was one covenant people, the nation of Israel. The figures used in the New Testament to describe the church are all pictures of essential oneness. The church is described as the family of God, its members are brothers and sisters, it is one body of which Christ alone is the head. Togetherness is not a subject we can afford to neglect or be indifferent about.

The quest for unity is an honourable one and it must go on. The work of the Holy Spirit in making the unity of believers possible does not minimize our own responsibility in seeking to maintain it. Unity may be produced in us by the Holy Spirit, it must be actively preserved by us.

Also in paperback from Kingsway . . .

Spirit Life

---

by Stuart Briscoe

What does it mean to 'live in the Spirit'?

Stuart Briscoe shows how we can fulfil God's purpose by allowing the Holy Spirit to produce fruit in our lives. To know love, joy, peace, patience, kindness, goodness, faithfulness, meekness and self-control, two things are required:

Our readiness to obey God's word; and our dependence on his Spirit to help us.

But how does it work in practice?

In his own engaging style Stuart Briscoe combines careful study of the Scriptures with personal experience and practical suggestions, showing how we can all reflect more of Christ's character in our day-to-day lives.

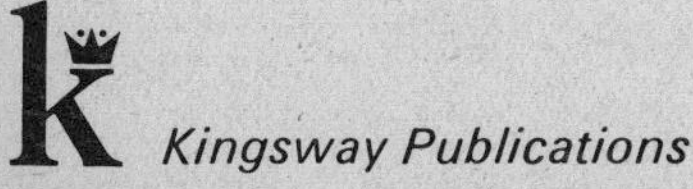

How to Fail Successfully

by Jill Briscoe

Failure is forgivable—not final

Does the fear of failure prevent you from stepping out in faith, or from witnessing to your family and friends?

Do those so-called 'little' sins rob you of the victory you know you should be enjoying in your Christian life?

Take heart, says Jill Briscoe—failure is not the end. Coping with failure, and learning to overcome it, are part of God's plan for all his children. Christians are not yet made, but in the making.

Jill Briscoe, in her own warm and witty style, gives practical insights and encouragement in her speaking and writing ministry around the world. She and her husband Stuart Briscoe, well known for their ministry in this country, now reside in the United States with their three children.

k

Kingsway Publications

The Darkness Where God Is

by David Gillett

Northern Ireland — the land that God forgot?

No, says David Gillett. The media's presentation of a violence-stricken land without hope is not a true, complete picture.

David has spent three years in the province and has seen at first hand the Spirit of God working in the hearts of both Protestants and Catholics. Out of his experience comes this book, which shows that there is more to Northern Ireland than bigotry and bloodshed; that the gospel of Christ has made remarkable progress despite the deep-seated attitudes of many that hinder God's reconciling work.

Above all this book gives Christians in Britain a new opportunity to pray and so join in the spiritual battle for Northern Ireland.

Kingsway Publications